D1552819

"Michael Gehring not only surveys critical and persuasively applies a spiritual indictm which has sometimes missed opportunitie: ing, right action, or what the faith community identifies as righteousness. Like a socially interested and passionate reporter, Gehring issues a series of prophetic challenges to the reader on a wide range of essential debates involving public theology and the sustainability of human community."

—VERGEL L. LATTIMORE III,
Hood Theological Seminary

"In a season of pandemic, a seasoned pastor reflects on his life and ministry forced into isolation. . . . Gehring surveys the history and current signs of deterioration and incivility in our social, religious, and political spheres. . . . In a time of cultural and political upheaval, Gehring yet proclaims his hope in a God who will deliver us and bring renewed life to the church, our nation, and our world."

—CHARLENE P. KAMMERER,
Bishop, The United Methodist Church, retired

"With a refreshing mixture of candor and hope, Michael Gehring's memoir of church life in these tumultuous times elicits laughter and tears. In these pages, we feel the church struggle and writhe, much as Jacob wrestles until he gets his blessing. Without shying away from politics, pandemics, or denominational turmoil, Gehring's account allows us a glimpse into the future where God is making all things new, and we dare to hope for God's work to continue through us."

—ROBIN CREWS WILSON,
Interim Lead Pastor, First United Methodist Church, Dothan, Alabama

"With his usual eloquence and accuracy, Michael Gehring helps us relive the peculiar and painful period of 2020 to the present. Using his own journey and theological reflections, Mike brilliantly weaves insights from great spiritual thinkers, ancient and modern, in a way that helps us all, especially United Methodists, untangle the knot of denominational divide, pandemic, and racial upheaval."

—ROB FUQUAY,
Senior Pastor, St. Luke's United Methodist Church, Indianapolis, Indiana

LOSING CHURCH

Losing Church

The Decline, the Pandemic,
and Social and Political Storms

MICHAEL J. GEHRING

Study Guide by Joe A. Hamby

RESOURCE *Publications* · Eugene, Oregon

LOSING CHURCH
The Decline, the Pandemic, and Social and Political Storms

Resource Publications
An Imprint of Wipf and Stock Publishers
199 W. 8th Ave., Suite 3
Eugene, OR 97401

www.wipfandstock.com

PAPERBACK ISBN: 978-1-6667-3459-1
HARDCOVER ISBN: 978-1-6667-9062-7
EBOOK ISBN: 978-1-6667-9063-4

JANUARY 7, 2022 10:17 AM

For All the Laborers in God's Vineyard
and in Memory of Harley Dickson
and Billy Abraham
Mentors and Friends

Contents

Preface

This work is a pastoral memoir reflecting on the decline of the mainline denominations, on the crisis of the United Methodist Church as it wrestles with same-sex marriage and the ordination of self-avowed practicing homosexuals, on the effects of the pandemic on the institutional church, and on the impact of social and political storms on congregational life. If you are looking for a recipe for church growth, this book is not for you. It is not a how-to-manual providing three easy steps to reverse the more than half-century of decline in worship attendance and membership in the United Methodist Church.

This memoir is a long lament that does not find redemption in bricks and mortar or other institutional concerns, nor in magical concoctions by Church Growth gurus, management consultants, or in saccharine motivational speeches by anxious church bureaucrats. It is so easy to be seduced by heartfelt speeches to "save the institution" that we begin to judge them to be an adequate or even justified substitute for the work that Christ mandated: teaching and preaching the Gospel, baptizing, celebrating the Eucharist, and making disciples of all nations. But as the Preacher of Ecclesiastes might have said, such speeches are another form of vanity and border on idolatry.

John Wesley, in his Twelve Rules for preachers instructed, "You have nothing to do but to save souls."[1] In this divisive and hate-filled time, there are many troubled souls that need saving from the bitterness of ecclesiastical conflict. They also need a north star to guide them through the truculent American political culture which offers up its own idols as saviors. Those troubled souls needed to know during the crushing isolation of the

1. *Doctrines and Discipline of the Methodist Episcopal Church*, ¶ 127.

pandemic that the community of Christ could help them weather the storm. Unfortunately, too often this was not the message that was communicated.

The broadcast and print news reporting on the church, more times than not, recounts the conflicts and divisions of Christian denominations. An outsider peering in would wonder, did Christ enter human history so that people would have ammunition for waging war over any number of issues that congregations and denominations divide over? One wonders if the image of organizational Christianity, as portrayed in our culture, is now a hindrance for the unchurched to meet the Risen Lord. The power and might of the institutional church developed over a long time, and God will certainly have the final say over whether it has been faithful to Christ's intentions or not.

The bride belongs to the bridegroom and Christ will have a church. The church two or three generations from now may not have salaried clergy, staff, and other professionals, nor will it necessarily have buildings. The church, in previous ages, has prospered in just such circumstances. Perhaps God is leading us into an iconoclastic age where institutional idols are deconstructed. The decline of the church may very well be leading us into rediscovering the Gospel.

This memoir captures aspects of the life of one United Methodist pastor in a year that none of us will quickly forget. By no means am I suggesting that this is more than one person's perspective, yet my hope is it will resonate. Frederick Buechner, the Presbyterian pastor and acclaimed author, wrote, "My assumption is that the story of any one of us is in some measure the story of us all."[2] Likewise, the story of any one local church is in some sense the story of all congregations. In many ways, this memoir is a love letter to the United Methodist Church and beyond. It is written in a style that is meant to be accessible for the laity and the clergy, and it is intended to facilitate needed conversations. Ultimately, this long lament finds its consolation in the sacred story and the mysterious work of God.

The burdensome, difficult year was made lighter by the incredibly talented team of pastors, staff, lay leadership, and congregants that I was privileged to co-labor with. God has called so many amazing and gifted servants to serve in the fields of our Lord.

I am indebted to Jeanna Bullins, Ron Cobb, Laurel Eason, Rob Fuquay, Keith Gehring, Jennifer Bingham Hampton, Jeff Hittenberger, Andy Langford, Wanda McConnell, Andrew Roginski, Will Willimon, and Robin

---

2. Buechner, *The Sacred Journey*, 6.

Crews Wilson for reading and critiquing various drafts of this work. The mistakes within it are mine, but there would be so many more if it were not for their efforts. Thank you to Joe Hamby for the labor of love in composing the study guide.

Like so many previous generations have already endured, we experienced a seismic disruption that broke into our lives challenging, frightening, and humbling us. Very few of us expected a global pandemic like the one we found ourselves navigating. Amidst the shutdown, we had the opportunity to examine how we were living our lives before the outbreak of COVID-19. The pandemic stopped us in our tracks, leaving us with more questions than answers. I invite you to travel along with me on a journey through a year that was unlike any other in my three decades of pastoral ministry.

Chapter 1

SANDS IN AN HOURGLASS

ON MARCH 1, 2020, we, the community called Main Street United Methodist Church in Kernersville, North Carolina celebrated the Eucharist. As the ushers directed, congregants and visitors lined up at the various stations to partake of the Lord's Supper. With hands cupped and outstretched, they came forward, and the pastors and the Eucharistic assistants broke off a piece of bread from one of the loaves, handing it to the congregant while speaking the words, "The Body of Christ given for you." The *Corpus Christi* recipients took a few steps, positioning themselves in front of the person holding the chalice. Dipping the bread into the dark grape juice, they heard the words, "The blood of Christ shed for you."

After giving the Benediction, the pastors recessed, while the music played. We took our spots at the sanctuary doors so we would be ready to greet. And greet we did, with handshakes, hugs, and pats on the backs. We received them in return, as well, along with a few kisses on the cheeks for good measure. In this age so defined by the Roman Catholic sexual abuse scandals, clergy are hesitant to follow the Apostle Paul's admonition that we greet one another with a holy kiss, even though Paul encouraged the churches in Thessalonica, Corinth, and Rome to do so.[1] The Apostle Peter instructed the same.[2] Fear of being misinterpreted in the twenty-first

---

1. Romans 16:16, 1 Corinthians 16:20, 2 Corinthians 13:12, 1 Thessalonians 5:26.

2. 1 Peter 5:14.

century is never far from the minds of many clergy. At times, it can feel like Damocles' sword is suspended above one's head. But I find it wonderful to be the recipient of such kindness, love, and grace that is communicated with a kiss on the cheek.

There has been much written about clergy antagonists within congregations. One pastoral counselor dubbed individuals seeking to dethrone, to take down, to harm pastors, as "clergy killers."[3] Though it is true that clergy do have to navigate and deal with difficult personalities, it is also true that for the few individuals seeking power and control in a congregation, there are many more who love their pastors and churches and want the best for them. Yet, pastors feel the heat and pressure increasing as institutional Christianity increasingly finds itself marginalized from the ongoing streams of cultural change in America. Church consultants, practical theologians, and denominational hierarchy continue to sound the alarm regarding the large number of ministers heading to the exit doors.

Some of those who cannot afford to leave the pastorate line up on Wednesdays and Saturdays in convenience stores purchasing Powerball lottery tickets and, for a few hours, feel a lightness in their souls as they dream of a life not constrained by economic hardship. Preachers who are morally opposed to the lottery find other ways to cope. Some indulge their escapist fantasies by immersing themselves in books, movies, and TV shows of an age that no longer exists. One of my favorites is *Grantchester*.

There is no shortage among United Methodist preachers of Anglophiles. The program's setting is a 1950s Cambridgeshire village named Grantchester. The Anglican priest, Vicar Sidney Chambers, and his successor Vicar William Davenport, are known by all and loved by many. The Vicar is so vitally relevant to community life that he assists Detective Inspector Geordie Keating in solving one mystery after another. For such a sleepy little town, it does not lack in murders. But what is important to notice is that in the Grantchester world, culture and power structures still support the institutional church. The church is culturally relevant and central to the life of the village.

On that first Sunday in March, standing at the doors of my church, basking in the fellowship, I could not visualize a scenario in which we would not celebrate in-person Communion as a community gathered in the sanctuary again, until the first Sunday in the following October. Seven long, fearful, anxious months later, while the pandemic still raged, we

---

3. Rediger, *Clergy Killers*.

congregated there again. This time, no common loaves or chalices were used. In the narthex, everyone was given his or her very own, self-contained, pre-packaged wafer, and pre-filled cup. They are, according to the distributor, hermetically sealed and easy to open. During the filming for the weekly Thursday devotion, I attempted to demonstrate just how simple they are to open. Struggling with one while the camera fixed its eye upon me, I finally set it aside and said with a smile, "Well, maybe not so easy to open."

By the first Sunday in October, so much had changed. So many aspects of worship we once took for granted were gone; masks were mandatory, temperatures were taken before entering the narthex, and everyone provided contact information. Ushers directed people to socially distanced seating; people who had occupied the same pew with their friends for decades were dislocated. No congregational singing was allowed and no handshakes, hugs, or kisses before or after the service. On March 1, if you had narrated such a pandemic story as we were living by October 4, I would have guessed it to be from some dystopian novel.

By March 8, things had changed just slightly. We had heard about this new virus, SARS-COV-2, we were instructed to refrain from shaking hands and giving hugs. On that day we were not asking, what did President Donald Trump know about the coronavirus and when did he know it? We were not asking whether the President had known how deadly the virus was in January. We were not wondering if the government was sacrificing public health to keep the economy propped up. The Ides of March were then a week away, and we were acting as if this virus were like the common cold. Knowledge was trickling down to us from the Executive Branch Office like sands struggling to make their way through a much too narrow neck of an hourglass.

On the eighth day of March, no masks were required, no social distancing, no temperatures taken, and no contact information provided. That afternoon, we gathered for a workshop in the Fellowship Hall. It was a packed house. Amy Coles, the Assistant to the Bishop, explained *The Protocol of Reconciliation and Grace through Separation*, which was proposed legislation for the General Conference that would meet in Minneapolis from May 5 through the 15, 2020. That was the hot topic of the moment, not COVID-19.

Amy explained that the United Methodist Church has been discussing and debating homosexuality since 1972. The denomination, founded in

1968 in Dallas, Texas, resulted from the merger of the Methodist Episcopal Church and the Evangelical United Brethren Church. Separation and unification are patterns repeated throughout Methodist history. The Methodist Episcopal Church founded in 1784 had numerous separations branching from it: The Republican Methodist Church in 1792, the African Methodist Episcopal Church in 1816, the African Methodist Episcopal Zion Church in 1821, the Methodist Protestant Church in 1828, the Wesleyan Methodist Church in 1841, and a few others after that. But the seismic shift, like tectonic plates crashing into each other, occurred in 1844. It was an issue of conscience, an issue of ethics, full of economic implications. Southern Methodists owned slaves. Even a Southern Methodist bishop owned other human beings. The Northern Methodists could not abide by such a departure from the teachings of John Wesley, the founder of Methodism.

Wesley, an abolitionist, also a friend and mentor to John Newton and William Wilberforce, loudly proclaimed his opposition to the vile slave trade. The Southern Methodists, unwilling to condemn human trafficking, lacked the motivation to work to abolish what the father of Methodism so vocally detested. Here were the Southern Methodists, a people who were moving on to perfection (supposedly), blatantly participating in, and profiting from, slavery. The Methodist Episcopal Church South, during the Civil War, adopted as its name the Methodist Episcopal Church in the Confederate States of America. When the war ended in 1865 and the country was reunified, the Methodist Episcopal Church North and South did not follow suit. Old feelings linger long. Old grudges are not easily released. Finally, in 1939, the Methodist Episcopal Church reunited, dropping the words of North and South.

The Evangelical United Brethren Church is itself the result of a union between the United Brethren in Christ and the Evangelical Church. The United Brethren roots are in the German pietistic movements of the eighteenth century. Philip Otterbein and Martin Boehm are the founding fathers of this denomination and its first bishops. The United Brethren were strongly opposed to slavery and, in 1837, declared that slave owners could not remain as members of United Brethren congregations. Likewise, a German ethos pervaded the Evangelical Church. Jacob Albright was its first bishop. This denomination also experienced divisions and mergers.

Some might think that the United Methodist name was chosen because of a shared denominational DNA that fuels and unites it for mission and ministry. That would be compelling, if only it were true. Others say that our denominational name is a typo and should have been called more accurately the *Untied* Methodist Church, which would certainly reflect the ideological conflicts present in the denomination since its beginning.

Albert Outler, the famed Southern Methodist University professor, served as the theologian of the new denomination, which embraced theological and doctrinal pluralism. And now, after all these years of conversation, debate, and conflict, the issue of homosexuality continues to divide. One cannot begin to imagine the pain that this has caused for the LGBTQ communities. Nor should one minimize the pain that this long-standing conflict has caused for some who hold to the traditional Christian teaching on marriage. Neither side believes the conflict and division is good for the church, yet the impasse remains. Every General Conference came and went without a solution that appealed to both sides.

In 2016, the General Conference voted to create another special task force charged with attempting to find a way forward that would hold the denomination together while allowing for a diversity of views and practice. Their proposals were defeated by the Traditionalists in the Called 2019 General Conference that met in late February. No compromise was achieved, and the Progressives viewed the actions of the General Conference as uncharitable and mean-spirited. The General Conference voted to double down on the enforcement of dissenting clergy and bishops who disregarded, as a matter of conscience, the rules in the *Book of Discipline* that prohibit the ordination of self-avowed practicing homosexuals and forbid clergy from performing same-sex marriage ceremonies. The conservative side of the church had its own litany of grievances, having endured its share of acrimonious accusations and demeaning characterizations. General Conference 2019 ended in a most bizarre way, and, to some, a rather fitting way; there was no time for a final doxology, because the Monster Trucks were coming into the arena.

Finally, after all the agony of the General Conference in Saint Louis was over, a realization settled in upon some in leadership, like fog in a valley, that the United Methodist Church is not going to be able to see its way through to an agreement that all sides can live with and, harkening back to the nineteenth century, perhaps the only way forward is to travel separately.

Back at Main Street UMC, as the Bishop's Assistant explained the Protocol, the existential crisis of the denomination weighed on my heart as I considered how my own church would vote, knowing full well that we, like the denomination, would also be divided. Once, we (United Methodists) considered our diversity a strength, and we celebrated in denominational publications a wide spectrum of political, religious, and philosophical views. Now, ideological differences play out in the culture and the denomination like armies clashing in the night. Some, but I am not one of them, think our diversity is our Achilles's heel. Pastors fear the carnage that could possibly occur. Like so many other congregations, Main Street UMC will not be of one mind. We will have a certain percentage of ardent Progressives, a larger percentage of Centrists, and perhaps the largest group of all, Traditionalists.

Main Street, like most other southern United Methodist congregations, has belonged to four denominations: the Methodist Episcopal Church founded in 1784, the Methodist Episcopal Church South (1844), the Methodist Episcopal Church (reunited 1939), and the United Methodist Church (1968). Now I wondered, which new denomination would my church choose? If we split into three denominations—Progressive, Centrists, and Traditionalists—I knew that Main Street would certainly not choose the Progressive option.

The divide over homosexuality has been a difficult storm for pastors to navigate. How many sermons have been given by shepherds goading their herds to love one another and to treat each other with the dignity and worth that a child of God deserves? Yet, all around the country and world, ministers have heard congregants letting emotions get the best of them, speaking uncharitable rhetoric in meetings with words that cut like a dagger into the hearts of their fellow brothers and sisters in Christ, some of whom are closeted, some of whom are open, and others who have LGBTQ children and grandchildren.

Why this issue? How does this one issue, with all the many problems of America and the world, rise to the top, supplanting all the others? Why is homosexuality the issue that generates the heated responses? Methodists are relatively quiet over a host of other issues: economic injustice, systemic racism, usurious payday and title loans, banks charging exorbitant interest rates on credit cards, an unjust tax code, the immigration crisis, pharmaceutical companies distributing opiates like candy, global warming, and a runaway military-industrial complex. President Dwight Eisenhower, a former Five-Star General, in his farewell address, did his best to warn the nation against the dangers posed by an unchecked defense industry.

United Methodists are rather silent on these issues, yet we are willing to divide the church over whether two people who love each other can make life-time commitments to one another in United Methodist congregations. The LGBTQ is left wondering, "Does my church want me to live a life of loneliness, or does it want me to live a lie?" No wonder so many Millennials are walking away from institutional Christianity. When C.S. Lewis, as a teenager, embraced atheism, he was by no means a reluctant atheist. Many Millennials are more than eager to lose denominationalism.

When I shared with the congregation the Sunday after General Conference 2019 what the denomination's legislative body decided on this contested issue, there was visible relief among some and anguish among others. A heaviness pervaded the room over what has been lost. *The Way Forward* would not have required congregations or clergy to perform same-sex marriages. Rather it extended the possibility of unity in the midst of diversity: a Georgia congregation could vote not to permit same-sex marriages to be performed in their sanctuary, and a congregation in Oregon could vote to authorize them. *The Way Forward*, if approved, would have allowed for contextualization of practice. It would have provided space allowing for different interpretations and practices.

On March 3, 2019, I preached on the lectionary text of Luke 9: 28–36, which is the mountain top experience—Transfiguration—and Peter's desire to remain in the land of glory, rather than to descend into the valley that would eventually lead to the *Via Dolorosa*, the way of suffering. I shared with the congregation that, by this point in the journey, the disciples had already seen Jesus cast out unclean spirits, heal Simon Peter's mother-in-law and countless other people of various kinds of diseases, calm the wind and the sea, raise the dead, and feed five thousand (not including women and children) with just five loaves and two fish. The ushers of that Galilean feast did not count the women and children because they were raised in a culture and time that often failed to consider women and children. But Jesus fed them; they counted in his mind and heart. Women, children, and outsiders all mattered to Jesus. About eight days prior to the mountain top experience, Jesus questioned his disciples and asked them, "Who do the crowds say that I am?" They responded, "John the Baptist; but others, Elijah; and still others, that one of the ancient prophets has arisen." He then asked them, "But who do you say that I am?"; Simon Peter answered, "The Messiah of God."[4] Jesus then sternly ordered them not to tell anyone. After that Jesus shared what he must endure and what discipleship entails.

---

4. Luke 9:18–20 (NRSV).

Jesus forecast storms, rock strewn roads, and dangers from religious and political powers that the disciples would experience if they kept following him. He did not mince words, making it clear, that the way forward would include suffering. Eight days later, three of the apostles experienced a theophany, a vision of God. On that day, Jesus, Peter, James, and John walked up the mountain to pray. While Jesus prayed, he changed before their eyes. His face became shining white. The veil parted. The three apostles were able to see that there is more to reality than what we normally behold.

Peter, overwhelmed by what he had seen, suggested to Jesus that they could build three dwellings, one each for Jesus, Moses, and Elijah. Perhaps Peter wanted to make the experience last a bit longer by building shelters and remaining on the mountain beholding the glory. When you have seen something that wonderful, it must be difficult to leave it behind and descend to the lowlands. However, the journey awaited: Jerusalem and Mount Tabor, agony and joy, the cross and the resurrection.

On that post-General Conference Sunday, I also shared the story of Johnny Cash and his Near-Death Experience (NDE). I recounted it partly because I am from Arkansas, partly because I am a huge Cash fan, and partly because it somehow related to the message I was giving. Well, at least, sort of. In preaching, sometimes, it is like horseshoes and hand grenades. Johnny Cash, troubadour of the badlands, once had an experience that he did not want to leave behind. It was 1988. While undergoing heart surgery, he had a NDE. Some say it is just the effects of anesthesia. For Cash, it was real enough. He saw visions of heaven and a bright shining light that beckoned him forward. He wanted to remain in that realm of spiritual bliss and was upset that he had to come back.

I suspect James and John felt somewhat that way too. They wanted to remain in that land of spiritual bliss and not travel down the mountain and onto the road that would eventually lead them to Jerusalem. Jesus had already told them that the Son of Man must suffer, be rejected, and killed. They knew danger lay ahead.

As I preached that day, I was mindful of how the LGBTQ community was enduring its own *Via Dolorosa*. They, who had built up such high hopes that after three years of strung-out conversation, would finally be accepted. They would finally be openly welcomed by the churches that they had invested themselves in and loved: hopes that they would not be rejected or condemned anymore, hopes that they would not be made to feel like they are outsiders or second-class citizens in the very congregations where they are helping to pay the light bills, salaries, building maintenance, insurance, office supplies, and all the many other expenses that these congregations incur, hopes that this time, it would be different; the clouds would part, and they would stand in the glory of full acceptance. This would be their transfiguration moment when their oppressive past is transformed into a hopeful future.

As I preached, I beheld a couple on the second row, tears flowing. Their Millennial daughter had told them that she, so wounded by the denomination's legislative body, would not be able to attend her home church for some time. She said, "I can't come back to church right now. I'm just too hurt and angry."

There was other hurt in the room that day. Though I saw relief in the eyes of many conservatives, I did not see any triumphalism. Those who opposed same-sex marriage were in pain as well. They hope for a day when their church heals from division and conflict, but they also do not want their church to engage in practices which they consider unbiblical. Those who breathed a sigh of relief were not of one mind. Some were grateful that they would not have to leave the congregation they love. Others, who could make allowances for same-sex marriage, feared that if that gateway were opened, the rushing waters of the progressive left will overtake their denomination. They feared that the surrender of the traditional teaching on marriage is just the beginning of a long erosion of Christian Doctrine that would eventually lead to denying the physical resurrection of Jesus from the dead and capitulating to modalism replacing the Trinity from "Father, Son, and Holy Spirit" with "Creator, Redeemer, and Sustainer."

There has not been enough discussion of the predicament of the centrists who could make room for same-sex marriage but overall lean theologically conservative. The centrists who lean right fear that whatever promises of restraint that are made now will be overturned when the evangelicals depart, and the progressives are left with far more clout. The Irish poet, William Butler Yeats wrote, "Things fall apart; the centre cannot hold."[5] The fear of the centrists who lean theologically right is that the center will not hold, that the big tent of United Methodism will be transformed into forced uniformity. The right-leaning-centrists are not comfortable with the progressives or the conservatives and feel adrift in the storm. When I preached the services that day, there was a lot of hurt in the sanctuary and

---

5. Yeats, *The Second Coming*.

in the chapel. They all wanted to know how a transfigured Christ spoke to their pain. They had long since left the glory of the mountaintop.

A year later, listening to the Protocol on March 8, 2020, and reflecting on General Conference 2019, I wondered if the time had now come for the warring factions to bless each other and go their own way. Congregations will lose people ideologically left and right. The denomination, of one's choosing, will not be progressive enough for some and not conservative enough for others. It is the fairy tale of Goldilocks and the three Bears being replayed repeatedly in churches across America. Pastors are hoping for more than a remnant who will say, "And this one, this particular assembly of believers, is just right." Pastors will be left attempting to reconcile budgets with declining revenues, all the while hearing comments about the good ole days. Pressures will be put upon pastors, by church leadership, to grow the church back to where it once was. The reality is, once this shift has occurred, once we move into a new age with its new paradigms, pastors will have more than their share of grief. They will not be alone. The laity too will feel like they are losing church; that church they once knew and loved will be in transition to the church it will become.

Chapter 2

THE STORM BEFORE THE STORM

CHURCH PEOPLE LOVE TO talk about the good ole days. For some, that means when their favorite preacher pastored their church. For others, it harkens back to the days when the pews were packed, and the offering plates were full. Mainline Christianity's glory days were post World War II America. The GIs returned home, hungering for normalcy and stability, and began rebuilding their lives, communities, and country. Theologians graced the cover of *Time* magazine: Karl Barth, Reinhold Niebuhr, and Paul Tillich.[1] High Church Evangelists were also featured: C.S. Lewis, an Anglican layman, and Fulton Sheen, a Roman Catholic priest.[2] Those glory days were not to last.

1. Karl Barth (1886–1968), a Swiss German pastor, theologian, and professor, is regarded by many as the most influential and significant theologian of the twentieth century. During his Safenwil years, he staunchly advocated for worker's rights and because of that was known as the "Red Pastor." As a public theologian, he vocally opposed the rise of National Socialism and Adolf Hitler. Reinhold Niebuhr (1892–1971), an American pastor, theologian, and professor, was also a champion of workers' rights. Niebuhr opposed American isolationism that sought to keep the United States from entering the Second World War. Paul Tillich (1886–1965) was a German American theologian who had a profound impact on American religious thought. When Hitler came to power in 1933, Tillich was dismissed from the faculty of the University of Frankfurt for his opposition to National Socialism. Niebuhr played a significant role in helping Tillich secure a position at Union Theological Seminary in New York.

2. C.S. Lewis (1898–1963) was one of the most significant lay evangelists and apologists in the twentieth century. He taught for many years at Oxford University before

The 1950s rebuilding of society gave way to the 1960s social turbulence, questioning institutional authority, and the generational battle cry of not trusting anyone over thirty. The decline of the mainline denominations from the 1960s until now has been unrelenting. The message and posture of these denominations in the 1950s conveyed confidence. Three decades later, in the roaring and prosperous 1980s, mainline denominations were riddled with anxiety, self-doubt, and haunted by questions of institutional survival. There were questions such as: Two generations from now will our denominational doors still be open? Forty years from now, will our local congregations still be able to teach and proclaim the faith to our children and grandchildren? Or will our churches be museums to the past, like the Shakers?

In a 1994 editorial in *Theology Today*, Thomas Long disclosed a conversation that he shared with a journalist who said, "American Christians ought to be scared as hell."[3] What was the reason for this ominous warning from this seasoned journalist? He answered, "little Christians are simply not growing up to be big Christians any more."[4] This was not the first alarm bell to sound. By that point, the warning bells had already been ringing for some time. It was, "All hands to the deck, the great sea going vessels are taking on water." In 1986, *Newsweek* brought the mainline decline to national attention in an article entitled, "From 'Mainline' to Sideline: Once the religious establishment, liberal Protestants are losing their sheep."[5] The subtitle stated the predicament succinctly. In 1920, 76 percent of American Protestants were represented by the seven mainline denominations; by 1986, the number had declined to roughly 50 percent.[6]

Richard Wilke, who at that time was the United Methodist Bishop of Arkansas, in his book *And Are We Yet Alive?* wrote: "We thought we were just drifting, like a sailboat on a dreamy day. Instead, we are wasting

---

taking up a professorship at Cambridge. Fulton Sheen (1895–1979) was a bishop and archbishop in the Roman Catholic Church. He was in the eyes of many protestants, the Roman Catholic Billy Graham. Of course, it needs to be said that Sheen was engaging in mass media evangelism when Graham was still in primary school. Sheen hosted a radio program on NBC from 1930 until 1950. He then moved to television and his show *Life is Worth Living* had a viewership of more than thirty million.

3. Long, "Beavis and Butt-Head Get Saved," 199.
4. Long, "Beavis and Butt-Head Get Saved," 199.
5. Woodward, et al., "From 'Mainline' to Sideline," 54–56.
6. Woodward, et al., "From 'Mainline' to Sideline," 54.

away like a leukemia victim when the blood transfusions no longer work."[7] His book was a wake-up call to the sleeping giant, The United Methodist Church. By the mid-1980s, the concern over the decline of The United Methodist Church was so widespread that Methodists took action in the 1984 General Conference held in Baltimore. To reverse this trend, the thousand delegates of the General Conference voted on a motion which, if implemented successfully, would have taken the United Methodist Church from over nine million members to over twenty million members by 1992.[8] The illusory resolution passed. The decline continued.

When reflecting on the mainline decline, the numbers can seem massive and impersonal, yet each number reflects a person who has left a local mainline congregation. In 1987, William Willimon and Robert Wilson, in their book *Rekindling the Flame*, stated that the membership losses of these five mainline denominations [The Episcopal Church, The Christian Church (Disciples of Christ), the Presbyterian Church USA, the United Church of Christ, and the United Methodist Church] in the 1970s and early 1980s accounted for a weekly loss of five thousand people, which would be like closing a seven-hundred-member church daily for fifteen years.[9] If every day of the week for a month, a local church of seven hundred members disappeared from one's community, the Christians of that area would be up in arms over the devastating problem. However, when it is a slow attrition on a national scale, it is more difficult for the average church attendee to recognize the severity of the problem. Willimon and Wilson wondered what effect such a long-term loss would have on the self-image of the clergy and laity of these once prominent institutions. Obviously, the impact is profoundly oppressive and far reaching. It is almost like a force of nature that one seems powerless to affect; as they state, "Decline is not a way of life, but of death."[10]

In 1989, Richard Ostling, in an article in *Time*, wrote that between the years from 1965 to 1989 when the United States population grew by 47 million, the five mainline denominations declined by 5.2 million.[11] Possible explanations for the decline were given: the inability of the mainline adults to pass on their faith to the young, the liberalization of their private colleges,

---

7. Wilke, *And Are We Yet Alive?* 9.

8. Wilke, *And Are We Yet Alive?* 26.

9. Willimon and Wilson, *Rekindling the Flame*, 12, 15.

10. Willimon and Wilson, *Rekindling the Flame*, 16.

11. Ostling, "Those Mainline Blues," 94.

the political gap between clergy and laity, foreign missions downplaying proselytizing, local churches avoidance of making converts, not developing significant presence on radio and TV, declining birth rates, demographics shifting, and a failure to attract "switchers."[12]

Once, the mainlines could count upon the switchers. In a quest for societal upward mobility, the switchers would transfer from a Pentecostal, or country Baptist church for the downtown, or suburban prominent socially respectable mainline church. But suddenly, the mainline lost its allure and many no longer felt being mainline was necessary for upward social respectability.

In 1993, Kenneth Woodward in *Newsweek* returned to familiar territory in, "Dead End for the Mainline? The mightiest Protestants are running out of money, members and meaning."[13] The membership of the United Methodist Church had fallen in 1992 to 8.7 million. By the 1990s, no one could deny the width and the depth of the mainline crisis. Stanley Hauerwas, the famed ethicist of Duke University, said, "God is killing mainline Protestantism in America, and we goddam well deserve it."[14] Hauerwas's comment is not necessarily a headline one would want to run in a mainline denominational newspaper, or as a sermon title in a church bulletin. And certainly not, for that matter, as a marketing campaign. But Hauerwas captured the angst of the mainline crisis. While the 1950s had echoed confidence and strength, the 1980s and 1990s unfolded with the mainlines searching for answers for the decline. They had difficulty understanding how this could happen to them, and they were left questioning, "Do Hauerwas's words possess more than an inkling of truth?" Some mainline laity and clergy pondered it. Others quietly left by the backdoor.

The decline continued into the new millennium despite denominations, regional bodies, and local churches employing consultants, demographic wizards, corporate strategists, and marketing gurus attempting to diagnose the problem and to offer what they considered as remedies. Church growth institutes, magazines, journals, and conferences could not reverse the decline. Megachurches of the moment created their own leadership conferences to teach pastors, staff, and laity how they can follow the recipe and have a church that others envy. Somehow the commandment about not coveting gets a pass when applied to happening churches.

12. Ostling, "Those Mainline Blues," 94–96.

13. Woodward, "Dead End for the Mainline?" 46–48.

14. Woodward, "Dead End for the Mainline?" 47.

In 2017, Ed Stetzer, who occupies the Billy Graham Distinguished Chair of Church, Mission, and Evangelism at Wheaton College, wrote in *The Washington Post* an article entitled "If it doesn't stem its decline, mainline Protestantism has just 23 Easters left." The catchy title grabs one's attention and evokes a response. Stetzer offered a hopeful future for the mainlines if they correct their course, but he concluded the article with the ominous warning that 2039 is fast approaching. It is important to note that Stetzer's timeline calculation did not include a pandemic. It may take church analysts and consultants a couple of years to sort out how much the plague of COVID-19 accelerated that timetable.

The loss of these once vital churches creates tremendous grief. Anger is also unleashed. We want to know: who is to blame for this? It must be someone's fault. The responsibility for this mess must stop on someone's desk. When a plane crashes, an inquiry begins about possible pilot error. If a ship runs a ground or its hull is ripped open on jagged rocks, speculation arises about the captain and the navigation team. Who was in command of the ship and were they sober?

In 2007, my son John and I traveled along with a group of parishioners from First United Methodist Church in Lincolnton. We went on an adventure following in the footsteps of the Apostle Paul. I never will forget the devotional my thirteen-year-old son gave on one of the last days of the trip. Taking the Scripture passage of 2 Corinthians 11, John recounted the Apostle Paul's hardships of following Christ: shipwrecks, being adrift on the sea, beatings, riots, and stoning. John said that we really had followed in the Apostle's footsteps; he cited when we were caught in a university students' riot in Athens and chunks of marble had rained down from the sky. Police fired concussion grenades and deployed tear gas. The students were prepared, wearing gas masks, and carrying lit flares. We ran, taking shelter in a restaurant. John also shared when members of our group became sick and when others lost their way. Then he took note of the night when we thought that the ship we were on (the MS *Sea Diamond*) was going to sink, as it was tossed about by the wind and waves of the Aegean. The next morning, as we headed to breakfast, we overheard a couple of the crew members talking about how the rough crossing had been so unnecessary and how the captain did not know what he was doing.

Sadly, not long after we returned to Lincolnton, we heard on the news that the *Sea Diamond* on April 5, 2007, had run aground onto a well-marked volcanic reef off the coast of Santorini ripping a huge hole in the hull. The ship sank and tragically a father and daughter were killed.[15] Six years later, a Greek court convicted the captain of negligence.

Sometimes, tragedies do occur because of pilot or captain error, and this should not be minimized. In the wreckage of the mainline denominations, a search for accountability is to be expected. It should not surprise anyone that when such a massive loss of members occurs over such a prolonged period, there is no shortage of finger-pointing, seeking to ascertain who is to blame for the demise of these once prominent and powerful institutions.

An obvious starting point is the clergy, bishops, and denominational executives. Is this unmitigated decline due to the clergy? Some clergy, maybe even many clergy, spend far too much time and energy hoping for, dreaming about, and scheming to achieve their next appointment, charge, or church. When a pastor is frustrated with how things are going in the church, it is far too easy to dream of greener pastures. The majority of clergy, unlike Benedictine monks, do not make a vow of stability.

Is it the bishops fault? Have they spent way too much time crisscrossing the country for denominational meetings and pet projects, attempting to escape the difficulty and drudgery of their pastoral work, shepherding the shepherds? What about the denominational executives? The clergy and the laity wonder, what exactly do all those denominational executives do in the first place? What difference are they making in the lives of congregations?

What about the theologians? Did they spend all their time working to serve the guild and not the church? Many theologians wrote for the academy, composing for other scholars, employing jargon, dazzling with multiple language citations (Greek, Hebrew, and ancient Hittite), reveling in esoteric thought that possesses little relevance for the person in the pew struggling to get through the week. This charge of negligence against the theologians is not new. C.S. Lewis leveled similar accusations against that profession many years ago.[16] Lewis claimed that if the theologians had done their proper work there would have been no need for one like him to engage in his project of theology for the laity. Do the seminaries escape the accusations? They are the ones entrusted with training the future leaders

15. The father and daughter were Jean Christophe Allain (age 45) and Maud (age 16), both French citizens.

16. For a discussion of C.S. Lewis's concerns about theologians, bishops, and priests who fail to adequately conduct the work proper to them see my book *The Oxbridge Evangelist*, 203–221.

of the church. And what about those who demand entertainment from the pulpit? Some laity hunger for fast-acting simple sugar and eschew protein.

There are multiple questions that need to be addressed to groups and individuals when they are placed in the dock. Questions include the following: Why are we declining? Has the Gospel lost its hold on human hearts? Is the problem the way that the message is being presented? Is the Gospel no longer proclaimed in a way understood to be faithful to the traditions of the apostolic teachings of historic Christianity? Some conservatives have pointed to Dean Kelly's book, *Why Conservative Churches Are Growing* as if it were the last word on the subject. Some traditionalists have used the decline of the church as a weapon against the bishops, the hierarchy of the church, and the clergy, claiming that the teaching of Liberal theology is responsible for the emptying out of the pews.

Conservatives have often failed to put the Gospel itself in the dock and ask, "Why is the Gospel not resonating more with this generation?" Even more to the point, not enough have asked, "Have we constructed a Gospel in our own cultural and political images that is a stumbling block to younger generations? Does our contemporary Gospel possess little similarity to the first-century rabbi named Jesus who so challenged the power structures of the day that the Roman authorities executed him?" Sedition, treason, threatening the social order were charges leveled at Jesus. He died as a criminal of the state deemed by Pilate to be King of the Jews. "We have no king but the emperor," the chief priests answered.[17] It was Pilate's job to ensure that remained true.

The preceding paragraphs about clergy, bishops, denominational executives, laity, theologians, and seminaries are caricatures, verbal cartoons, and portraits which are cursory and unsatisfying. Seeking to cast blame on others only further divides the church and fosters suspicion and hostility. The clergy and the laity have wanted, with very few exceptions, their denominations and congregations to flourish. Outliers exist, a few Samsons, reveling as they push down the pillars of the Temple, but the great majority of preachers and parishioners have sacrificed for their churches. Pastors, attempting to be faithful, have embraced different church growth paradigms, even though the storm seemed unrelenting. Like Sisyphus, they have been pushing the boulder up a mountain. Many clergy have sacrificed their health and their families, attempting to push back a massive weight which seems inevitably determined to continue its course.

17. John 19:15b (NRSV).

Perhaps, we are scapegoating for some of the same reasons that the ancients did. If we can locate where the blame resides, then, metaphorically speaking, we can be like Phinehas and save our village, tribe, and people from God's divine wrath, the plague.[18] Maybe in our zeal to correct whatever we believed to have gone wrong, we hope to court God's favor again. This decline has got to be someone's fault, does it not? It cannot be just sociological and cultural changes, right? It cannot just be that there are far too many entertainment options, and that society is moving away from valuing the church, can it? We, who have crafted our own idols of the institutional church, are we perhaps holding on too tight?

It is simplistic to point the finger at any one entity, or person, or groups, and say, "Ah, that is the reason why." It is also callous to deem the decline of mainline Christianity as a punishment from God. I do not believe that all mainline churches will disappear in nineteen years, but some will. Perhaps, even many will. That, in and of itself, is troubling for those of us who love the church.

18. Numbers 25:6–15.

Chapter 3

RUINS AND RESTORATION

As I SAT LISTENING to the Bishop's Assistant on the eighth of March discuss the implications of *The Protocol of Reconciliation and Grace through Separation,* my mind wondered, "How many of the clergy are going to experience this proposed legislation as possessing any similarity to reconciliation or grace?" Certainly, from the viewpoint of the pastor in the trenches, it will not seem harmonious. It is not a secret that mainline clergy, by and large, lean further left politically and culturally, than many of their congregants. When the congregations leave who are hard right, what will become of their clergy who are politically and theologically to the middle or left? What will be lost when the congregations and preachers resemble each other? What spiritual dynamics will be lost when the preachers and congregations are homogeneous? What would the early church have been like if no space had been provided for the inclusion of the pagans, the Gentiles, and it had simply remained a movement of Jewish Christians? Would there even be a church if the Judaizers had won the day?

As I muddled this over in my mind, a memory from the previous year surfaced. On May 17, 2019, at the invitation of President Vergel Lattimore, I had the privilege of giving the address at the Honors Awards and Closing Convocation for Hood Theological Seminary in Salisbury, on the eve of graduation. I took for my text the first thirteen verses of Chapter One of the Book of Haggai. I wondered what of Haggai's experience of attempting to rebuild out of ruins would speak to these freshly minted Master of Divinity graduates entering into perhaps their first full-time appointment and, at the same time, resonate with seasoned pastors who are graduating with their Doctor of Ministry degrees?

Thus, I said to the assembled, "I imagine that some of you are wondering why I chose such a dramatic text as Haggai's for this occasion? You may be sitting there thinking our homelands are not in ruins, our churches have not been destroyed by foreign armies, leaving not one stone upon another. Everywhere we look is not desolation and sacrilege." I then shared with them that the reason why I chose the passage from Haggai about rebuilding amidst the ruins is due to the existential impact a particular book made upon me nineteen years ago. I am a bit of a geek, and I have read much through the years, so it begs the question: How could one book make such an impact? Stan Menking, for the course *Reaching the Unchurched*, assigned *Death of the Church* by Mike Regele and Mark Schulz.[1] I would not have read it except under duress. They wrote:

> The institutional church in America will look very different twenty-five years from now. Indeed, several denominations may no longer exist. We are sure that there will be hundreds of local congregations that won't. The forces reshaping our culture are too many and too strong. We see signs of social fragmentation and collapse everywhere.[2]

The authors, demographic wizards, had the numbers to corroborate their prognosis. *Death of the Church* was published in 1995. I read it in January of 2000. My first thought was, "Five years have already gone by. The church cannot die; I invested in the Pension Plan. I am only thirty-eight. I have three children and a wife to support. I have no other skills." Regele and Schulz put me in a funk, and I said to the graduates, "I hope that I am not putting you in one as well."

I continued, "These are odd times in which we abide. Mainline denominations are splitting. The United Methodist Church is trying to navigate some difficult terrain without dividing, but we do not know how it will turn out. It is too early to tell. It is peculiar times in which we live, but it was also strange times when the prophet Haggai lived."

Some commentators say Haggai's name means "festive" or "my holiday" or "to make a pilgrimage." It is thought that he may have been born

---

1. This was part of the coursework for the Doctor of Ministry degree in Evangelism at Southern Methodist University.

2. Regele and Schulz, *Death of the Church*, 11.

during one of the pilgrimage feasts. Some say he was an old man who still remembered the glories of Solomon's Temple before its destruction by the Babylonians. Now, he is calling the people to let go of what is past and together build a new future and a new place for the people to worship God.

I said to the graduates, "The Church in America also needs to let go of its idols and idolized past." I continued to share with them that we do not live in the post-war boom of the 1950s that some equate with the "glory days" of institutional American Christianity. Those halcyon days were not as glorious as people make them out to be. Voices were stifled and excluded, just as today. In that supposedly golden age, segregation ruled the day, women were relegated to bringing casserole dishes to church suppers, and nationalistic fervor led by Senator Joseph McCarthy of Wisconsin ruined the lives of artists, writers, political activists, and others, with false accusations of the twentieth century scarlet letter: a red C for Communist.

By no means am I saying that there were not traitors amongst us in those days just as there are today; but the hype and hysteria instigated by a P.T. Barnum wannabe brought ruination to so many lives. Perhaps one of the greatest traitors of all to American values of fair play, good will, respect for others, and breathing free air without fear, was McCarthy himself. Slander, false charges, and bold-faced lies need accountability when they are espoused by political leaders. In those "glory days," the bomb shelter building business prospered while children learned to "duck and cover" under their school desks. In that pinnacle age "in God we trust" was printed on our paper currency yet it appeared that the nation's real confidence lay in developing the hydrogen bomb and other weapons of mass destruction. Fear of the other continued through the ensuing decades: fear of minorities, fear of immigrants, and fear of the powerless demanding a new deal for a new age.

I shared with them, "The mantra of my seminary (Princeton Theological Seminary) was *Ecclesia reformata, semper reformanda*, which means a church reformed and always being reformed." That challenge remains before us: reformed and always reforming. That should be true not just for my alma mater, not just for the Presbyterian Church, but for our cities, states, and country. How do we honor the good of our past, honor the heroes of our nation, and yet still be able to name our national sins without being branded as un-American? How do we honor those people who take a knee protesting injustice and still honor those who stand for the flag? How do we resolutely oppose the idolatry of certain politicians who want to convince us that they have the solution for all our problems? We are not yet the people God desires us to be as individuals, as communities of faith, or as a nation. We too, people in the United Methodist tradition, need to take a cue from our brothers and sisters in the Reformed tradition and embody the church, reformed yet reforming.

That evening, I told the graduates, "It is a new day, and God is doing a new thing. Old forms and structures may need to go away. What is dying is not God's church but forms of cultural Christianity that we have lived with for a long time and in which we have become too comfortable. The call upon your lives is greater than a cultural crisis. The God who called you to this place, to this moment of time, is greater than any storm that blows. And the storms are certainly raging."

I continued, "Though it is true that we do not live in a land where foreign armies are destroying our churches, we do live in a land where churches are intentionally burnt down. We live in a land where people gathering for prayer in God's houses are shot dead in cold blood. We live in a land where hatred consumes human hearts. We still live in a land full of broken dreams and shattered lives. We live in a land suffering under a plague of prescription drug abuse, substance dependence, and other addictions. We still live in a land needing the healing that only God can bring." Concluding I said, "God has gifted and anointed you. God will have a church, and you all are privileged to be God's chosen instruments to help bring about repentance, reconciliation, redemption, and restoration."

Two months short of a year after that address, sitting in the Fellowship Hall, hearing about *The Protocol of Reconciliation and Grace through Separation*, I wondered how many of those graduates feel so blessed to be in this moment when the United Methodist Church is about to rend itself in two or three. In that moment, it became as real to me as it ever has been, in the three decades worth of working in the fields of the Lord, that none of us went into ministry to maintain crumbling institutions. None of us went into ministry to hear the soul-crushing refrain, "Make more bricks without straw." None of us went into ministry to save a denomination that clearly treats some people like they are second-class citizens.

We went into the ministry to save and care for souls. We went into the ministry hoping for a new day when the lion and the lamb will lie down together. We dreamed of a new age, when the church will stop accommodating itself to the culture, stop prostituting itself for political relevance and prominence, and truly become the liberating Gospel that speaks truth to power and seeks to build a more just world. We dreamed of a new day, when the Church will join together attempting to remedy the immense social and relational problems of our very broken world. We went into the ministry so that we could be vessels, so that God could fill us full of these new dreams for a better day.

The laity come to church, not for ecclesiastical disputes but to hear a liberating Word from God. They come to church to be encouraged, to be equipped, to be strengthened, so that they can be, like Teresa of Ávila wrote, "the hands and feet of Christ." Yet too often, what we clergy do is to fill the slot of committees of the church with names of people, engaging in a bait and switch. How often have we been the architects of a less than fulfilling deal? Instead of helping our congregants to find transcendence, we put them on the Worship Committee, where they will experience the worship wars of the traditionalists versus the contemporary crowd. Instead of engaging them in the *Missio Dei*, transforming hearts and society by the power of God, we place them on the Endowment for Missions Committee so that they will endure the soul wearing debate of whether the allocation of resources for mission work should be only locally distributed or can some funds possibly go beyond the borders of one's hometown, state, and nation. Instead of helping them to build the Kingdom of God on earth, we deposit them into the Building Committee on an expansion that is unnecessary and lacks the funds to sustain it. Yet, the conversation ensues because the church down the street just completed a fabulous addition. The Lord's prohibition against coveting, in church circles, thus does not seem to apply to ecclesiastical buildings.

As Amy concluded the workshop, I grieved the conflict in the denomination and knew that the way forward must include providing space for different theological positions on a topic that is nowhere as clear cut as the progressive or the conservative position portrays. When the meeting was over, after the goodbyes were exchanged, my wife Rhonda and I headed home.

Chapter 4

Northward Bound

On March 8, 2020, there were five hundred known cases of the coronavirus in the United States, and North Carolina had two of them. There were a good number of states that did not have any. When I write that COVID-19 was not on our radar in any significant way on March 1, I am not suggesting that the media had not been reporting on it all along. We had heard reports about travel restrictions. We knew about the heroic Dr. Li Wenliang, a Chinese Christ figure, who gave his life attempting to alert the world to the frightening danger of this brand-new virus. Wuhan bureaucratic machinery attempted to silence the physician they labeled a "whistle-blower" and a "rumor monger," censuring him and forcing him to sign a letter of admonishment.

The media reported on all of that and countless other stories. The headlines of that time were about the front-runners of the Democratic Primary: Bernie Sanders versus Joe Biden. There were stories about the upcoming March Madness tournament and other athletic contests—stories of geo-political maneuvering in Afghanistan with the Taliban—stories about Syria and the Russians—stories of China and global prominence—stories about immigration and border patrol—stories about whatever tweet that President Trump had typed that day.

For more than three years, the United States endured a president who seemed to thrive on division. In so many ways Trump's presidency resembled a TV reality show and in other ways it appeared to have more in common with the WWE (World Wrestling Entertainment). Like Ric Flair boasting, Trump had no problem making the presidency about himself. For more than three years, America heard a president brag that he knew more about ISIS than the generals, that he knew more about politicians, social media, or just about anything else than anyone else. Trump was never shy about stating that he graduated from an Ivy League school.[1] For more than three years, America had suffered from the Trump's messaging that created division, alienation, and broken relationships.

By no means am I suggesting that politics has not always been a rough business. There are plenty of examples of rancorous comments and dirty tricks played in every generation stretching back before the founding fathers of this country. But technology took the game to a whole new level. What responsibility does Facebook, Twitter, and other social media platforms have for the apparent disintegration of constructive political discourse?

What perplexed me was the open-hearted embrace of Trump by many Evangelicals who had rained down condemnations on President Bill Clinton's indiscretions. A consistent position for the ultra-right Evangelicals would have been to condemn not only Clinton's actions but also Trump's. In my three decades of pastoral vocation, I had not witnessed before so many Evangelical far-right Christians turning a blind eye to a president who engaged in blatant distortions of reality and truth, as if he were the one who defined what was true and false, what was right and wrong. The far-right leaning Evangelicals appeared as if their moral compass needed to be remagnetized. Trump seemed to be encased in Teflon, and many Evangelicals lionized him, not holding him accountable for his words and deeds. High-profile evangelists and megachurch preachers cloaked themselves in Trumpian garments. Just as in the days of the prophet Jeremiah, religious leaders willingly played the role of court prophets, blessing and sanctioning corruption.

When we returned home from the Protocol workshop that Sunday afternoon, not much time passed before Rhonda and I registered our fatigue. I said, "Let's postpone our departure for a day." She agreed. Monday marked the beginning of her spring break from the Iredell Statesville School System. We had been planning for some time to travel to New Jersey to visit our son John in Wrightstown. Since he was in a relatively new job and had

1. Trump graduated from the University of Pennsylvania with a bachelor's degree in 1968.

little vacation time accrued, we understood that we would only be able to see him in the evenings. We booked ourselves in a hotel off Route One in Princeton so that during the day we could revisit our old stomping grounds of Princeton Theological Seminary and Westminster Choir College.

Busying ourselves around the house on Monday getting ready for our trip, we took care of last-minute details. Toward evening, looking at my emails, I read that Princeton University had announced the move from in-person to virtual education. Stupefied by what I had read, I stared at the iPhone. I heard no conversations Sunday morning from parents of Demon Deacons, Tar Heels, Wolfpacks, or Blue Devils that their university students would be soon coming home. I then read that Governor Phil Murphy of New Jersey had declared a State of Emergency. Wondering if New Jersey was experiencing a different reality than we were, I said to Rhonda, "Maybe this coronavirus is a little more serious than we thought. Should we cancel our trip?" She, a public health nurse, who wanted to see her son, said, "We will take plenty of hand sanitizer with us and use it liberally along the way." For some reason, masks were not even part of the conversation. Though I did not watch 60 *Minutes* the evening of March 8, I viewed it later, hearing Dr. Anthony Fauci, the Director of the National Institute of Allergy and Infectious Diseases, state, "Right now, in the United States, people should not be walking around with masks." He also instructed the elderly to avoid large crowds.

The award-winning journalist Bob Woodward, in his book, *Rage*, detailed that on January 28, of the year that we now refer to as pandemic year, President Trump was told by Robert O'Brien, the National Security Adviser, "This will be the biggest national security threat you face in your presidency."[2] Matt Pottinger, the Deputy National Security Adviser, agreed with O'Brien. Pottinger's sources had been telling him that one should not think of this new virus from China like one thought of SARS 2003, but more like the deadly influenza pandemic of 1918, which had killed more than 50 million people world-wide and more than 675,000 Americans.[3] Knowing all of this, Trump continued to tell the American public that "they faced little risk."[4] His attention, according to Woodward, was focused on almost everything except the virus. On February 2, Trump declared to

2. Woodward, *Rage*, xiii.

3. Woodward, *Rage*, xv.

4. Woodward, *Rage*, xvii.

Sean Hannity of Fox News, "We pretty much shut it down coming in from China."[5]

On March 10, armed with plenty of hand sanitizer and not a single mask, we departed later than we had anticipated for New Jersey. The day before we leave on any lengthy trip, without fail, I will pontificate, "Tomorrow, let us depart before the sun rises so that we can beat the traffic." Without fail, our departure time falls between 9 and 10 am, just as it did that Tuesday, heading toward the Garden State. We made our way to Business I–40 heading toward Greensboro. We passed the time talking as I–40 Business merged onto I–40 E and then eventually onto I–85 N.

I brought along Barbara Brown Taylor's book *Leaving Church*. I had first read the book when it came out in 2006. I thought so highly of the book and her previous work, especially *The Preaching Life*, that, some years later, I emailed her and invited her to headline First United Methodist Church's Heafner Preaching Mission, Lincolnton. She responded politely declining my invitation, citing the need for more time for solitude, more time for prayer and centering, and more time for writing. She said that she was in a season of turning down many preaching invitations.

I felt a little bit like those first century Galileans and Judeans who kept hungering for more of Jesus even as he skillfully evaded them, disappearing into the wilderness for solitude and prayer.[6] I could hear one of those first-century denizens say, "Of course, Jesus, we understand. By all means, you need to take some time away. We want you to do that. Just take care of our needs first and then you can go on along your way to your land of retreat. Well, our needs, our neighbors' needs, and that of some guy whose name I forgot and never met, but my wife told me about earlier this morning. She actually asked me to check on him but since I do not have a clue who he is, and since you are who you are, you can do that for me, can't you?"

Luke wrote in his Gospel, "But now more than ever the word about Jesus spread abroad; many crowds would gather to hear him and to be cured of their diseases."[7] The word spread; the needs were plentiful, and the throng of the hungry, destitute, sick, depressed, needy, grieving, hopeless, and abandoned never let up. Jesus did one of the soundest things that a

---

5. Woodward, *Rage*, xvii.

6. See Matthew 14:23, Mark 1:35, 6:46, Luke 4:42, 6:12, 9:18, 9:28.

7. Luke 5:15 (NRSV).

healer can do when used up; he withdrew from the crowds and went to a deserted place to pray.[8]

Will Willimon, in his book, *Pastor*, quoted Stanley Hauerwas, who said that contemporary pastors are a "quivering mass of availability."[9] These "quivering" pastors did not start out that way. What needs accountability is how congregations and denominational systems reward workaholics, who are always available to tend to their congregation's needs even if it means that the minister's spouse and family feel neglected, overlooked, and taken for granted. What needs further attention is how congregations become critical of pastors who draw boundaries, taking the full extent of their vacation time and refusing to leave their families at the beach in order to return to conduct a funeral for a parishioner who died while the pastor was away. Jesus enforced boundaries that would get him fired by many American congregations.

I wanted to respond to Barbara Brown Taylor, "Really, time away. What's that like?" When I let loose those vowels and consonants, "really, time away," it sounds like a bugle call summoning to action. However, if you examine my calendar from any given year, you will find that I reliably maintain that boundary. It saddens me to see wonderful friends not willing or able to employ such boundaries. Too many of them have been raised in family systems that taught them to be pleasers and thus are beaten down by congregations' expectations.

The lamentation of "time away" is evoked by pastors in the trenches across the land. Nothing strikes coveting more in a pastor's heart (well, except that is, someone winning the Powerball Lottery) than to know of another pastor who found a way to break free from the continuous refrain that haunts pastors' thoughts: "Sunday is coming, and I have got to find something to say. But I feel like I am all out of words." Air Supply can sing and make money about being all out of love, but preachers are in the word and meaning business and to be at a loss is a vocational crisis. Sunday is coming, and feeding the sheep is leaving the shepherd hungry and depleted.

Rhonda is fond of saying, "Nurses have a bad habit of sabotaging one another." There is a syndrome among some nurses of being the "Super Nurse" who never takes a break and out works everyone else. I have heard the same is true of teachers and social workers. Why do the helping

8. Luke 5:16.

9. Willimon, *Pastor*, 60.

professions foster and reward this behavior? Ministry is not an exception, and ministers are often critical of other ministers.

I wrote Taylor back and said that I understood and was envious of her resolve to enter that sacred space of prayer, solitude, and writing. Then I said a prayer acknowledging my envy and communicating that I hope it is true that God will accept me just as I am. Though that hope hangs more on a song by a Long Island poet than it does on any passage found in the Scriptures.[10]

I chose as one of the books for our congregation's 2019–2020 monthly book club *Leaving Church*, which we were scheduled to discuss on March 19. I wanted it fresh in my mind for our group discussion so I asked Rhonda if she would read it aloud as we traveled northward. As we passed the next state's welcome signs, we were reminded that Virginia is a place for lovers. Rhonda, in her northern South Carolina accent with echoes of Appalachia, began to read the Introduction.

Barbara Brown Taylor begins *Leaving Church* by noting how she intended to mark the twentieth anniversary of her ordination in the Episcopal Church. Ordained in the month of May, she hoped to observe the anniversary by spending time in a monastery or if not that, at least, devoting some hours to contemplative prayer. It does not escape my attention that though many protestant clergy seem attracted to monasteries like a moth to a flame, I had labored to get free from one.[11]

Somehow, someway, the day marking Barbara Brown Taylor's ordination got away from her. I suspect that statement could characterize many of our lives. Somehow time just gets away despite all our day planners and best intentions. Perhaps she spent the time at the college where she now teaches; perhaps the day passed on her farm. Even though the day went by without her formally observing it, I am impressed that she remembered the date of her ordination. I have no idea when Bishop Richard Wilke ordained me as a Deacon, nor do I have a clue when Bishop Bevel Jones ordained me as an Elder. I would check on the ordination certificates, but they are wrapped in bubble wrap and stored in a taped-up box in the garage. It is amazing the items that are framed and proudly displayed when one is young, and yet, as the years pass, no longer see the light of day.

10. Billy Joel, *Just the Way You Are.*
11. See Gehring, *As the Broken White Lines Become One*, 28–32.

I am struck by Taylor's use of the word "spent" in connection with the passage of a day. I cannot help but think of John Milton, the seventeenth century poet, who at one time studied for the Anglican priesthood. He penned the line: "When I consider how my light is spent."[12] Most scholars believe Milton wrote the sonnet between June and October of 1655. It is also held that Milton went blind in 1652. Blindness could not stop Milton from his God-given appointed task.

As preachers exit from the local church or when they draw near to retirement, many of them also wonder, how have they spent their light? Did they make a good choice investing in institutional Christianity? It is an investment that Jesus never made. Jesus did not endure lengthy finance committee meetings wondering, "How will we close out the year? Will we be able to make payroll and pay our denominational obligations?" When Jesus needed money, he simply told Peter to cast out a fishing line and pull a coin from the mouth of the first fish that he caught.[13] Would not that be a neat trick sure to impress any church leadership board if the average vicar could pull it off? Furthermore, Jesus never rushed through traffic to get from one hospital to another to visit the sick. He simply said, "Be healed."

Obviously, that pain of late-night finance meetings, propping up a declining institution, or fighting rush hour traffic to make hospital calls cannot compare to the crucifixion. By no means am I suggesting such a comparison, just stating an observation that we all know to be true. Jesus never had to organize a church potluck supper. He simply said a prayer over five fish and two loaves and fed a crowd possibly as large as the weekend worship attendance of a massive megachurch. Jesus does possess some similarity to the mainline denominations, but, of course, he exceeded them. The mainlines have been slowly losing members for more than half a century, and Jesus in a relatively short period of time witnessed his active participants decline from the size of a mega-church to just a handful of followers who were still loyal to him as he hung upon the cross. Trust me, Jesus never would have made the cover of *Church Growth* magazine. We have to leave that for the Holy Spirit on Pentecost.[14]

Long-entrenched preachers tend to second-guess themselves about whether they made a good decision to spend their lives in the ministerial

12. Milton, *Sonnet* 19.

13. Matthew 17:24–27.

14. Approximately three thousand were added to the new church on that day (Acts 2:41).

profession. Should they have rather started their own ministries, or gone to law school, medical school, become a stockbroker on Wall Street, or any other of a number of options? The preacher's sense of calling will be very relevant at this existential moment of angst. Even when preachers leave their parishes in the rear-view mirror—losing all aspiration to make bricks without straw—relishing in relinquishing responsibility for being institutional mid-level managers of organizations that the culture no longer supports, and in some parts of the country barely tolerates—they cannot help but live into their calling in a myriad of ways. As we go deeper into Taylor's story, we will see how that is true of her as well.

Barbara Brown Taylor shares with the reader that she no longer spends every Sunday preaching sermons. Now, on some Sundays, she visits churches of other denominations, listening to preachers struggling with words at the intersection of the vertical and the horizontal, that crossroads of the eternal and temporal, striving to bring meaning, challenge, and comfort to haggard souls, or to others that are far too at ease in Zion, comfortable souls reassured by their education and breeding that God is lucky to count them in the Kingdom. Sometimes, enjoying the freedom she now has, released from the constraints of the collar, Taylor spends Sundays sipping Assam tea on her front porch. What was that prohibition about coveting again?

Listening to Rhonda read these words, my mind drifted to the seventeenth century metaphysical poet and Anglican priest, George Herbert, who in his poem *The Collar* wrote, "My lines and life are free, free as the road. Loose as the wind, as large as store."[15] What preachers sometimes forget is that they are not the only ones dreaming of open roads that lead to less complicated lives. Donald Justice, a twentieth century American poet, wrote about men at forty softly closing doors.[16] Of course, as a pastor, I have heard too many stories of doors closing, sometimes quietly, and other times slammed so hard the house shakes.

On Sunday morning, plenty of minds are roaming, closing doors on their youthful years, yet still yearning for wide open spaces with new adventures and beginnings. Maybe even hoping for new jobs, spouses, cities, and states. Of course, with the nonsense and divisiveness of Washington, DC, in the Pelosian and Trumpian age, probably more Americans than we know dream of moving to new countries, all the while the preacher sermonizes

15. Herbert, *The Collar*.

16. Justice, *Men at Forty*.

on duty and responsibility. Sometimes parishioners' minds fantasize about choosing what is behind Door Number One or Two or Three or, for that matter, any door that would lead to a new land populated with fresh hopes and aspirations.

Taylor refused to settle for unactualized dreams and, in the coming chapters, will tell the story of how she exchanged a church pulpit for a university lectern, of how she traded the collar and other ecclesiastical trappings for the wardrobe of the laity. The vestments that she once wore now proudly hang in a Kenyan Anglican Church sacristy. In telling her story, she will recount her search for real life through the three distinct seasons of the faith: finding life, losing life, and finding life again. It is the archetype that Jesus embodied and gave to the Church. There is no road that leads to an empty tomb that does not first go through the baptismal waters of the Jordan and then later to Golgotha. There is no final triumph for Jesus without death, and no ultimate joy without the Way of Suffering, the *Via Dolorosa*.

After Rhonda finished reading the introduction, she set the book down, took a sip of iced tea, and then began reading the first chapter. In the tenth year of her ordination as an Episcopal priest, Taylor knew a change needed to be made. She had grown weary in the ministry. She was one of four priests serving in a large downtown Atlanta church (All Saints' Episcopal Church). Her job responsibilities included visiting parishioners in hospitals and nursing homes and, in addition, fulfilling various administrative tasks for which she was responsible. She worked at a frantic pace to keep up, but the work simply repopulated itself. It wears on one: all these unfinished tasks, and the people behind them needing a healing touch from a priest. She thought God would keep making deposits in her account as she kept making withdrawals for others. Her husband Ed also got to a point where he too needed a change from the hectic Atlanta life.

They began making day trips out of the metropolis, seeking to discern if they could really live anywhere else but the city. They did not want to settle into the suburbs. They wanted something completely different, turning a whole new page, beginning a brand-new chapter. They wanted farmland in the countryside, some place where you could raise chickens and whatever you fancied. As they drove around for weeks, an idea settled upon them to locate in the mountains of northeast Georgia. Driving into a quaint village called Clarksville, population fifteen hundred, they knew it felt right.

Finding the town's Episcopal Church, Grace-Calvary, Taylor fell into love at first sight. Problematically, the church was not looking for a new rector.

The priest at Grace-Calvary was beloved by his people and was a local legend. But two days after All Saint's Day, he was found dead in his house. Three days after hearing of his demise, Taylor called the bishop and added her name to the list of potential candidates for this church that she now coveted. That had to be a weird phone call.

I remember sitting in the Fort Smith District Office meeting with Bill, the District Superintendent. A phone call came in that interrupted our meeting. My assigned mentor in ministry had died a few days before. After Bill had hung up the phone, he turned to me and said, "Well that didn't take long." "What?" I asked. And he replied, "A preacher just called wanting to put his name into consideration for First UMC, Paris." That was the church where my mentor had served. As a person fresh in the ministry, I felt in that moment that something profane had occurred. Looking back all these years later, I know how true it is that life moves onward; ceremonies are held, and gaps are filled.

After Rhonda finished the second chapter, we took an offramp to get some coffee, iced tea, and gasoline, fuel for both driver, passenger, and Pilot. As the Honda merged back onto the interstate, Rhonda began to read Chapter Three where Taylor describes how she anxiously waited for her new clergy shirts, collars, and brass-plated studs. The clothes represented the culmination of a long journey. She shared how she had fallen in love with God as a child, experiencing the divine outside in the fields behind her parent's house in Kansas. Her parents were not church goers, and she attended church for the first time at the age of seven. There she met God in the sanctuary, but not in Sunday School, where she found no connection between it and the Divine Presence.

When her family moved to Georgia, she continued to experience the Divine Presence while walking in the moonlight on the greens at a nearby country club. Her hunger for God remained in high school and in college. She majored in religion as an undergraduate. After graduating from Emory University, she traveled northward for her seminary studies matriculating at Yale Divinity School. During her second year at Yale, she started attending Christ Episcopal Church and discovered there a strong sense of the Divine Presence. After a period of discernment and mentoring by the rector, she joined the Episcopal Church and was later confirmed her last year at Yale. Following graduation, she returned to Atlanta and took a secretarial job at a United Methodist seminary. It took her five years to navigate and complete the ordination process. Finally, she reached the long-anticipated milestones and was ordained first to the diaconate and later to the priesthood. What she learned is that the collar changes everything. When you are set apart, you are truly set apart. People view and treat you differently. Sometimes that is wonderful and other times agonizing.

Rhonda took another sip of iced tea, and then began reading the fifth chapter. The Grace-Calvary search committee worked for almost a year sorting through résumés, and discerning which candidates looked like the best fit for their church. Grateful to learn that she had made the final cut, she worked on a sermon that she would preach for the prospective parishioners. On the appointed day, she did her best to "dazzle them." Hearing Rhonda read those words, I remembered why I am glad to be a United Methodist pastor. If it remained up to me to astonish a committee with my homiletical skills to gain employment, I never would have gotten my first job. I would probably, now to this day, be working at a beach somewhere serving umbrella drinks to tourists and writing bad poetry on cocktail napkins.

One morning, I stopped by the Fort Smith District Office, but Bill was gone. I spent some time catching up on district happenings with the secretary. She said Bill would chuckle and go on and on about how he was sending to Cavanaugh United Methodist a pastor (me) who had only preached two sermons in his life. Thankfully, the Bishop appoints a preacher to a congregation, and the church, despite its concerns and hesitations, receives him or her with grateful hearts. Well, at least, that is the ideal. Some preachers are met by grumbling souls yearning for another. On his first Sunday, one of my colleagues, after the service stood at the front door of the church shaking hands and greeting his new congregants. A parishioner, in his early thirties, looked down to his five-year-old son and said without smiling, "That is the man who is going to try to take the place of Preacher Rob." The newly appointed pastor smiled, swallowed his pride, and said, "I'm not Rob, but I'll do my best."

For Taylor, the long-anticipated day finally arrived. The phone rang. It was the Chair of the Search Committee. Taylor heard in the chair's voice both weariness and elation. Later, Taylor learned that some families, upon learning of her call to be the new Rector, had left the church because she was a woman. Then, like so many other clergy, she began to inhabit two worlds, the world she was leaving, and the world which she hoped would welcome her shortly. So many details to take care of before one moves and so much work to be done at the same time to prepare for the new world one will be entering all too quickly.

In that season, time seems to move, in one moment, like molasses and in the next like a rushing river. Eventually, Taylor and her husband arrived at their new rented home and started to settle in. She began in the church by cleaning her office and other rooms. Now looking back over a score and a decade of ministry and a good number of moves, I wish I had thought of that. That is a great idea both literally and metaphorically. Clean out the dust; clean out the ghosts. Of course, in church work, the ghosts never really do flee. Some former pastors never do really depart either. A colleague followed a pastor who had been appointed to a busy demanding church, yet he still found time to return to his old church for pastoral visits bringing along fresh baked pies. The new preacher thought, "I do not have time to turn my kitchen into a bakery." He wondered, "How am I ever going to be accepted?"

Leaving the busy large steeple urban church where a day planner was an essential tool (back in the days before the smart phone), Taylor acclimatized to a new rhythm of life. Parishioners did not call and make appointments. They simply stopped by the church whenever they wanted to meet the new rector. As the days turned into weeks, she began to learn the blessings and the challenges of pursing pastoral vocation in a small town. The collar does, indeed, set one apart, and anonymity is the stuff of preachers' dreams. She also learned that even in a small community, people with remarkably different views of life, varying positions on political and philosophical matters, find a way to live together. When she asked a newcomer why he chose to attend church there, he replied, "I know people who come to this church, and I finally had to come see for myself how they got through a Sunday morning without assaulting each other."[17]

As Taylor narrates her story and introduces the reader to the cast of characters that made up the congregation and the town, one hears in her voice a shepherd who deeply cares for her sheep, a shepherd who watches out, protects, leads, assists, and challenges those entrusted to her care. Yet, all of that care exacts a cost on the shepherd, and she wisely wrote that as long as she fed them, she did not feel her own hunger pains.

17. Taylor, *Leaving Church*, 66.

After renting for six months, Taylor and her husband began searching for land on which to build their new home. Eventually, they discovered a place where they felt the Divine Presence, where, as the Irish say, there are "thin places" that serve as portals connecting our world and the one beyond. Moving a manufactured house onto their new land, they waited expectantly for nine months as their home was built. Finally, the day arrived for the housewarming party, and the congregation gave them two rush-backed rocking chairs. Inviting them, so to speak, to sit and stay awhile, which they gladly did.

I drove, listening to Rhonda read *Leaving Church*, as cities came and went, Greensboro, Durham, and Petersburg. From I-85, we kept left and merged onto I-95 heading to Richmond, then past the District of Columbia, past Baltimore, as we continued our northward drive. When it became too dark to read, we turned on iHeartRadio and listened to the Bruce Springsteen channel: nothing but the Boss as we passed Wilmington, traveling north, seeing signs for Trenton, and eventually merging onto Route One heading to Princeton.

Chapter 5

THE ROARING EIGHTIES

PULLING INTO THE PARKING lot of the Hyatt Regency, 102 Carnegie Center, we took note of the ample availability of parking spaces. Something is up. It should not be this empty. After settling into our room, we walked to the Pilot and made our way to Washington Road as the Alexander Street bridge was closed. Motoring down Faculty Road, we did our best to take in the sights as the evening darkened. At Alexander Street, we turned right and journeyed to the Seminary.

My mind flashed back to days of playing Hacky Sack in the Quad as we graduate students in divinity talked about what an odd duck this or that professor was. We had no idea of the greatness surrounding us. Listening to pulpiteers and scholars who made it all look so easy, we cavalierly pontificated about who was up to snuff and who was not. One of our favorites was Johan Christiaan Beker, the famed New Testament theologian. We loved him because he was not button-down. As a youth, Beker was taken from his family in Holland by the Nazis and sent to work in a factory near Berlin. Amid the brutality of the Third Reich, the Allied air bombings, holding life by a prayer, with all of the loss, with all of the fear, he made the decision that one day he would be a theologian. Somehow, he managed to survive the war and graduated in 1948 from the University of Utrecht. He then traveled to the United States to continue his studies in New Testament, eventually receiving his PhD from the University of Chicago. Beker did not glibly handle the tough theological and scriptural questions, nor did he rush past them: "My God, my God, why hast thou forsaken me?" He wrote about suffering as one who not only endured it but continued to combat his own internal wars.[1]

No one at the Seminary doubted Beker's brilliance or his eccentricity. For his part, Beker had little patience with pretense. He had looked deeply into the nature of humanity and the reality of a fallen world. With a personality that loomed as large as his did, there were bound to be stories, and stories there were, although one never knew what was true and what was not. By one legendary account, years after coming to the Seminary, he, a full professor in an endowed chair, became so wearied by the everydayness of life, by the mundane, by the tiresome routine of academic life that he just disappeared. Days went by. Search parties were dispatched. Eventually, President James McCord, the larger-than-life Texan, found him working as a fry cook in Trenton, and simply said to him, "Christiaan, come home."[2] And so Beker returned to Princeton, a land too affluent, too comfortable for the internal wars in his soul. There were many other Beker stories, not that they were all necessarily factual. Student narratives have a life of their own. Sometimes the truth is nowhere as interesting or as fun as the stories embellished by graduate students in need of their own break from the prosaic.

Parking in front of Miller Chapel, I reflected on the truth of the novelist Alex Haley's comment about the turtle on the fence post. None of us got to where we are by ourselves. We are all indebted to others, and my list from those days is lengthy. It is also tempting when looking backwards to see it all through rose colored glasses. There were many good days, and some not so great, but is this not the way of life? Before leaving campus that March day in 2020, I checked my emails and read that the Seminary had announced that very day that they too were going virtual. Turning right onto Mercer Street, we rode slowly taking in the sights. We passed by the Princeton Battle Monument. Unveiled in 1922, it celebrates General George Washington and his troops' victory over the British in the Battle of Princeton on January 3, 1777. It also laments the loss of General Hugh Mercer, who perished in that fight. I welcomed seeing the monument again, grateful that a war memorial unveiled in 1922, was dedicated to something other than the Lost Cause whose statues populate small and large Southern towns and cities, including Statesville where I used to live.

1. See Migliore, "J. Christiaan Beker, A Tribute (1924–1999)," 96–98.
2. Garry, "A Heavy Gold Chain."

Turning right onto Nassau Street, my mind went back in time. It was the roaring eighties. Had F. Scott Fitzgerald walked down the street, you would not have thought him out of place. It was the decade of glitz, glamour, and greed. Ronald Reagan occupied the White House, and the bulls ran wild on Wall Street. Not being a descendant of robber barons, but just a poor seminarian, I needed to work while in school.

In those days, you could find me many nights and weekends behind the counter of Princeton Video Express at 20 Nassau Street. Now I know what some of you are thinking—a video store, how nerdy—but I assure you, back then, it was a happening place. Peter Benchley, who wrote the novel *Jaws*, was a regular patron, as was Brooke Shields. We had some great customers! There was the high-flying lawyer who frequently entered the store with a woman on each arm. He was dashing, personable, and fun. Sadness filled my heart when he went to prison. Apparently, some Mafia clients paid him in cocaine. Like I said, it was the raucous eighties.

The great majority of our clientele were wonderful. When you rang up their weeks' worth of late charges, they would just smile and say, "Put it on the card." There were a few who were indignant that rules really did apply to them and would argue and threaten, promising to report us to the owners, or other authorities of cosmic power. There were also a few who looked down their noses at clerks behind the counter, knowing full well that our names were not recorded in some blue-blooded registry, knowing most certainly that they would not find our pictures in the society pages of *The New York Times*. We had no shortage of pompous assistant professors and graduate students from the University who could easily have drowned in a rainstorm. People think the Ivy Leagues are all that until they live amongst them. Then scales fall from eyes, and human brokenness remains a constant.

I guess that is why I took such a liking to one of our customers. When he came into the store, he wore workman's clothes and shoes. I imagined he toiled long hours in a factory to take care of his family, especially living in an area where the cost of living was so high. He could not have been more considerate. I thought the world needed an abundance of people like him, my blue-collar brother, who understood what it was like to come from my humble roots. Neither one of my parents finished high school. Dad used to say that he graduated from the School of Hard Knocks.

I liked this guy. He was just as kind and ordinary as they come. I never paid much attention to his last name. It was all too common, kind of like

Smith or Jones. One day, while watching the evening news, I saw my working-class brother, except he was not wearing his industrial clothes. He was sporting a suit, surrounded by people dressed to the nines. He and his siblings were contesting his father's will. I saw my guy, my blue-collar brother, J. Seward Johnson Jr., standing there. The news reporter said that he was the grandson of one of the founders of Johnson & Johnson. My mind stuck in down gear, grinding like cognitive dissonance. Later, I learned that he was a famous sculptor, and his celebrated artwork could be found all over the world. It dawned on me then. I did not really see him. I cast him in a mold of my own making. I did not know that evening that he had passed, but a couple of days later I read in *The New York Times* that J. Seward Johnson II died on March 10 in Key West, Florida. The very day I am remembering him in Princeton, he is leaving the world in Key West.

We continued driving on Nassau Street past PJ's Pancake House and past Firestone Library. Looking to the left, I beheld Princeton United Methodist Church remembering back to the first time I entered those doors. My first year in seminary I did not have a car. When I discovered John Wesley while reading church history, I deeply resonated with his spiritual journey of how he a high church Anglican priest had his heart strangely warmed while hanging out with the Moravians. Furthermore, Wesley, taking the Gospel out to the coal fields and the inner-city slums, preaching, and doing works of mercy among the poor, the down-and-out, and to those that society overlooked or deliberately chose to ignore, struck a chord with me. After learning about John Wesley, I had to meet the people called Methodists and walked to the closest United Methodist congregation I found. I had no idea then what the future held for this denomination.

We continued driving making out way to Westminster Choir College. Westminster had fallen on hard times in the early 1990s. It was taken over by Ryder University, due to the Choir College not having sufficient endowment and revenue to continue its operations. Some decades later, Ryder had conversations with a Chinese company to sell the campus, but the plan was vigorously opposed by Westminster's alumni and others. The Chinese eventually withdrew their offer. At that time, March 2020, Ryder's plan was to move the Choir College to Lawrenceville, sell the Princeton campus, and in the view of some Westminster alumni, pocket the cash, like a corporate raider. Suddenly, like a flash from the past, it is Gordon Gekko all over again. Nothing stays the same, the old saying goes, and how true that is, when returning to your roots.

As we drove around Westminster, we tried to remember who we had been before raising three children, several dogs, goldfish, turtles, and any other creature that my son found. In that moment, we tried to recollect who we were before all the jobs we had worked, who we were when we began dating, who we were in a simpler time when our horizon was wide with possibility, and imagination roamed the landscape. We strained to recall who we were as carefree students unencumbered with responsibility.

After leaving the Choir College, we drove to the Wawa at the Dinky, or to use the rather elevated term on the map, the Princeton Train Station, picking up a few supplies. Returning to the hotel room, I turned on the news and caught the headlines and reports that I had missed driving north. Governor Andrew Cuomo had created a containment zone around New Rochelle, New York, due to its cluster of COVID-19 cases—one hundred and eight reported so far. New York City had thirty-six cases. In Washington state, the coronavirus had spread like a wildfire, and twenty-three people had already died from this new little-known virus. Many more were believed to be exposed. Italy's death count was soaring. Joe Biden and Bernie Sanders cancelled rallies in Cleveland, saying they would consult with public health officials before rescheduling large public meetings. The DOW Jones tumbled. Also in the news, two Russian planes were intercepted off of the coast of Alaska.[3]

As I laid my head down on the pillow, I closed my eyes and thought, just a week and two days ago, we were celebrating the sacrament with common loaves and chalices, feasting on the joys of community, shaking hands, giving hugs, exchanging kisses, and in our lexicon possessing none of words and phrases that would shortly become common: "shelter-in-place", "social-distancing," "contact tracing," "temperature taking," and "Zoom meetings."

On Wednesday, we drove to the Seminary's Gift Shop and picked up a few more drinking glasses etched with the Seminary logo on them. I had bought four of them two years prior when Rhonda and I attended the Alumni Reunion. Remnants of the class of 1988, we gathered to mark

---

3. I am a self-professed news junkie and during the COVID storm I imbibed far more broadcasts than I should have listening mostly to the BBC, CNN, the major networks, and Fox. Most of the news summaries in this work are indebted to NBC Nightly News with Lester Holt.

the thirtieth anniversary of our graduation. The glasses were on a table in my home office when our one hundred and twenty pound Akita, Charlie, kicked the footstool which hit the bookcase, that dislodged a framed photo of James Baldwin U.S. postage stamps that came crashing down, breaking one of my glasses.[4] After depositing them, we sauntered around enjoying a few photo-opts.

Climbing back into the Pilot, we headed to the Institute for Advanced Study, the site of one of our earliest dates, drinking hot tea on a cold night in the courtyard until the Security Guard chased us away. After exiting the Honda, we took pictures in front of the Institute's banner at the main building. Observing what we took to be geniuses walking about, fellows out for a stroll, we wondered what it must be like to be so intelligent that one is given keys to a club as exclusive as the one to which J. Robert Oppenheimer, Albert Einstein, Kurt Gödel, and Michael Walzer all belonged.

Christianity teaches that what God values most is not how smart, athletic, or beautiful one is. John Milton wrote that God does not need "Either man's work or his own gifts."[5] What God values, first and foremost, is faithfulness; living a soulful life that loves and values others; a life that treats all with the inherent dignity and worth that they deserve as children of God. The world's standards are different; and brilliance, in and of itself, without being anchored in a God-fearing soul, has created havoc, chaos, and great suffering in our world. C.S. Lewis made this point so well in *That Hideous Strength*.

The counterpoint to the previous sentences about the world's standards in contrast to the church's standards needs to be made. Christians have long laid claim to the mantle of Jesus's teaching. Evangelicals have portrayed to culture and society that they are the embodiment of it (one thinks here especially of Jerry Falwell Sr.) but, in the apex of the Donald Trump presidency, what needs to be called into account are the nationally known religious leaders and evangelists who turned a blind eye away from the President's behavior simply because he supported certain public policies to which they were aligned. The Evangelical far right, by and large, refused to speak out against Trump's loathsome caricatures of others, his callous policies, and his treatment of women. Yet all the while, they felt

---

4. James Baldwin, a twentieth century American writer spent much of his adult life in a self-imposed exile in France, attempting to flee the racism and homophobia of the United States. He greatly influenced many writers including Maya Angelou and Toni Morrison.

5. Milton, *Sonnet* 19.

entitled to their status as privileged spokespeople of that first-century Jewish rabbi named Jesus who said, "Blessed are the merciful, for they will receive mercy. Blessed are the pure in heart, for they will see God. Blessed are the peacemakers, for they will be called children of God."[6] The Evangelical Right's political and religious support of Trump created cognitive dissonance in many millennial evangelicals who could not reconcile the message of a first century itinerant rabbi with the raw political machinations of Trump and his disciples.

Not everyone has spoken of the rarified air of the Institute for Advanced Study in glowing terms. The renowned theoretical physicist, Richard Feynman, who completed his PhD at the University, said that when he was in Princeton in the 1940s, he saw what happened to the great minds of the Institute.[7] Here they were in this wonderful world with no demands placed upon them, no students, no classes, no departmental duties, just time and space for thought. Feynman referred to the fellows as "poor bastards," for once they got there, the ideas would not come.[8] There were no students to ask questions, no interruptions, and no challenges. For Feynman, it was the teaching of students, the give and take of that process, that kept him going.[9]

Leaving my ruminations on Feynman, I checked my emails and read the responses from the staff back in Kernersville to an email that I had forwarded from another congregation in our annual conference. The Senior Pastor of that United Methodist church wrote that he and his leaders were implementing new safety precautions for worship: no shaking hands, and liberal application of hand sanitizer. He also discussed that they might have to suspend Communion or else celebrate the Eucharist differently. This elicited a spirited response from one of my staff members who said that we should not, under any circumstances, stop using the common cup and loaf: my sentiments exactly. The Eucharistic meal without a loaf of bread and a chalice full of liquid grace seemed unimaginable. But now that I was in New Jersey, I knew that the landscape had changed in ways that I had not understood when I left North Carolina on Tuesday.

We drove through the cathedral of trees, continuing our way to the Graduate Tower and then back to the Seminary. We parked in front of Alexander Hall, took a few pictures, then made our way to the library. After

6. Matthew 5:7–9 (NRSV).

7. Feynman, *Surely You're Joking, Mr. Feynman!*, 191.

8. Feynman, *Surely You're Joking, Mr. Feynman!*, 191.

9. Feynman, *Surely You're Joking, Mr. Feynman!*, 191, 192.

viewing the current exhibits, we exited the library, heading on foot down Mercer Street and then onto Nassau meandering in and out of the stores until we arrived at the Triumph. We descended the hallway ramp that connects the street to the main floor of the restaurant, where there was a good-sized unmasked crowd.

Settling into a booth, I opened a copy of *The Daily Princetonian* and read to Rhonda the front-page story; on March 10, John Brennan was the first person from the Garden state to die from COVID-19. He was a sixty-nine-year-old man from Little Ferry in Bergen County. He had been hospitalized since the sixth of March. A horse trainer, Brennan had worked in Yonkers and made no trips to Wuhan. The paper also stated that the total number of confirmed cases in the state stood at fifteen. James Tedesco, the Bergen County Executive, encouraged senior citizens, especially those with chronic conditions, to avoid large crowds. *The Daily Princetonian* also reported that two University faculty members were being tested for COVID-19.

After lunch, we crossed the road, passing through the University gates, traveling back in time, taking pictures along the way of Nassau Hall, Firestone Library, the Chancellor Green, and of the University Chapel where I graduated so long ago. We continued to absorb the beauty of the University as we walked past statues of the Tigers, down the steps, through the University bookstore and out onto the street, heading to the Pilot that would take us to the hotel. Back in our room, we freshened up. It was late afternoon, and John would be getting off work in about an hour.

We departed Princeton, heading to Wrightstown. After picking John up at his apartment, we drove to the Sebastian Schnitzelhaus at 43 Fort Dix Street. Over supper, John told us about his work as a biomedical tech, repairing respirators. When the meal was over, he rated the food nowhere as good as Wiederkehr's Restaurant in Altus, Arkansas, to which Rhonda and I readily agreed. When the evening became late, we made plans for the next night. Hugging our son goodbye, we headed to the hotel. After returning to the room, I turned on the news to see what we had missed.

The DOW Jones had plunged yet again. The World Health Organization had declared the coronavirus outbreak a global pandemic. The news reported that there were now more than a thousand cases in the United States. More than a hundred universities announced they were ceasing in-person education. Students were being sent home and would have to finish the semester online. Travel from Europe was suspended for thirty days.

The NCAA announced that all sporting events would now be conducted in empty venues, without any fans at the events, including the NCAA Basketball Tournament. The NBA also stated that their games would be without fans in the arenas. Bernie Sanders had performed not as well as expected in the Tuesday primary but vowed to keep on fighting. Around the world, major attractions, including Vatican City, were closing to tourists.

Chapter 6

The Glory Days

In my first year in Seminary, Bruce Springsteen ended the *Born in the USA* tour on October 2, 1985. One of my seismic regrets is that while living in New Jersey, I failed to make it to a single Springsteen concert. That would have to wait until I lived in Charlotte. Another regret is that I never drove the short distance to Asbury Park, nor did I ever just show up on his doorstep asking, "Hey, do you want to write some lyrics together?" That was probably a good call. I imagine people who do that are gifted with a restraining order. Regardless of my failings in those regards, like Eric Church sang, Springsteen was a soundtrack to not only a hot July night but also to my teenage and young adult years. How many windy two-lane highways were burned up while the speakers blasted *Blinded by the Light*?

One would not need to spend much time where I grew up to understand why Springsteen's music resonated. Reagan's trickle-down economic policy did not bring showers of economic empowerment to my area. Just the reverse, as Reagan, in draconian fashion, cut social welfare programs. That is one of those matters that God will want to ask him about. Politicians appear to behave as if it is just some sort of sport, a game between two teams: the Republicans and the Democrats, the Reds and the Blues, the Elephants and the Donkeys. All that seems to matter is getting reelected and ensuring that your team is in control of the House, Senate, and the White House. All the while, the middle-class fall further behind, and the poor suffer indignities that should not be visited upon citizens of one of the richest countries in the world.

Reagan, or one of his handlers, co-opted *Born in the USA* for campaign rallies, all the while ignoring the painful truths to which the song gave witness. Reagan engaged in a massive spending increase for the military-industrial complex while cutting social welfare funds, resulting in, among other things, the deinstitutionalization of the mentally ill. Many of them, devoid of resources or safety nets, were forced to live and die homeless on our nation's streets. The far-right Evangelicals eagerly embraced Reagan and all that he stood for but failed to take seriously the crucified Messiah and how he continues to live in the ill, the disenfranchised, and the poor. Reagan repeatedly referred to America as "the shining city on a hill," but God's utopian vision is never built on the broken backs of widows, orphans, the destitute, the homeless, the hopeless, and upon those who cannot mentally, physically, or spiritually tend and fend for themselves.

Wall Street prospered in the Reagan age, but people in my hometown would continue to be challenged. Often, they would have to drive for up to an hour for work that, more times than not, was a factory job at a place like Cloyes Gear in Paris, or the chicken plant in Dardanelle, or Whirlpool, Rheem Manufacturing, Baldor Electric Company, Gerber Baby Foods, Dixie Cup, Planters, or Hiram Walker in Fort Smith. To get on at Cloyes Gear, it helped to know someone who already worked there. Even though employment could be found, the minimum wage was losing ground against the cost of living and there was a sense that things were not getting better despite all the rhetoric from Washington, D.C. Politicians, they say, campaign in poetry and govern in prose. People from my area desired to know if anyone had them on their radar.

Not long ago I emailed questions like these to Senator Tom Cotton's office. I wanted to know what economic development plans he had for the Arkansas River Valley. Cotton, a Harvard educated lawyer, is from Dardanelle. He grew up with the very people I am writing about. Our high schools competed against one another in football. I never really got a satisfactory answer to my inquiry. Of course, it does not help that I currently live in North Carolina and am not registered to vote in Arkansas. That was plainly and unceremoniously pointed out to me by one of his staff members. Though I continued trying to be heard, it was like talking into a hurricane. Cotton's constituent count is in the millions and form letters are the most that the average voter can hope for in response to expressing a concern or raising an issue.

The "fly over" states want to know that they matter as well. People in the 1970s and 1980s had already started to feel their hopes were slipping away or just beyond reach, wondering what their homeland would be like for their sons and daughters, fearful that the American dream no longer applied to them. The farmers struggled to afford the equipment needed to harvest the crops, and to cut and bail the hay so that the cattle ate during the winter months.

The well-fed bulls, however, were running on Wall Street, but I did not know anyone who worked on Wall Street. Mercy, I did not even know a single Edward Jones branch manager. Springsteen's songs, elevating the plight of the working poor, introduced me to people I already knew. These were the people of my homeland, hardworking souls who fought in America's foreign wars, shed sweat, tears, and blood, only to be left behind by the titans of corporate America. What of the American promise will there be left for their children and grandchildren? What jobs will remain for those born in the USA when the multi-national corporations send so many of them overseas to places like southeast Asia?

In 2007, I was privileged to be sent, along with a group of approximately twenty-four pastors from a leadership program within our annual conference to Seoul, South Korea, to study the discipleship structure and ministries of Kwang Lim Methodist Church. Kwang Lim is a church that has around a hundred thousand members. The church is broken down into small groups led by lay pastors; once a year, every family in the church receives a visit from one of the ordained pastors. It is a celebrated event when the pastor visits the home. They divided our group into subsets of three or four and took us to visit three families that represented a cross-section of the congregation: a wealthy family, a middle-class family, and a poor family.

In the afternoon of May 1, we began our visits. The first was to a wealthy family. The husband/father was a CEO who owned a factory in China, employing more than a thousand workers. He had left his downtown office so that he could be there for the visit with the church pastor and the three guest pastors from North Carolina. He bestowed on us beautiful gifts, and we gave them our humble offerings from the Tar Heel state. They lived in a beautiful skyscraper condo that overlooked the city. What he said stunned me. He commented that his workers are demanding more wages and that he is looking into relocating his factory to Thailand. Shocked, I asked, "You mean, it is cheaper to close down a plant, build another plant, equip it with all the machinery needed, than to just give them a raise." He said, "Absolutely." Of course, I understood his point of view as best as I could as one who grew up in small family-owned businesses. But I wondered, without government intrusion and regulations in business today, how can any worker ever hope for stability in the workplace?

Growing up, I did not know any of the privileged: the CEO's, bankers, lawyers, and doctors, though I went to school with their sons at a Roman Catholic Benedictine High School. Most of our students were from the South, but we also had students from Mexico, Latin America, Europe, and Iran. As a day student who did not live on campus, I stood outside their world. My hometown was not their hometown; my limited economic resources were not, by and large, their reality. I had no plans to go to college. It seemed too far a stretch for me, and I did not care for school that much anyway, which was supported by the comments that the monks made on my report cards. My plan, up until high school graduation, was to enlist in the Army and become a biomedical technician like my brother. Everything was set for him to come home the week after my high school graduation and be there for my swearing-in ceremony.

I do not know why, but the night I graduated from Subiaco Academy, I changed my mind and in time, everything changed. What I thought would be a lifetime of collecting ribbons on a uniform became an odyssey of accumulating far too many books. One of the reasons why I could choose to attend university is due to the Social Security program that enabled orphans to receive benefits until they were twenty-two. My father died when I was eleven. Reagan eliminated that program my senior year. What would my life have been if I had decided not to go to university? How would I have endured standing behind some assembly line job performing the same routine task seemingly into infinity? Of course, had I done so I would not now be worried about how to maintain a congregation in a declining, fracturing denomination.

On Thursday, we took NJ 133 to 33 and on into Freehold. We drove around the Township and the Borough while listening to, of course, *My Hometown*. Trying to visualize the father and boy driving around in the big Buick like proper citizens of their land, residents with dreams and expectations. Springsteen sings about the protagonist, the eight-year-old now grown up with his own son, wondering if he and his family will have to pack up and start over elsewhere. His hometown is not his father's hometown.

The jobs are being shipped overseas, and downtown is now a land of vacant buildings and vanquished dreams.

We stopped at St. Rose of Lima Catholic Church at 16 McLean Street and took pictures of the church. We also took a few selfies in front of the church. Springsteen and I share that Catholic culture, upbringing, and education with nuns, rules, and duties. We then made our way to 39½ Institute Street. I parked the car and said, "Let's go get a selfie in front of Bruce's old home." Rhonda said, "No, people live there." I thought, "It is not as if we are the first people ever to have a selfie made in front of that house." I asked again; she remained resolute. Rhonda stayed in the car. Holding up the iPhone, centering Bruce's childhood to high school home in the background, I smiled as I tapped the camera, capturing the moment.

We drove over to the Freehold High School and imagined the tension and fights between the blacks and whites in 1965, troubled times not only in Freehold but across the country, troubles that have not yet disappeared. We then motored to downtown and tried to visualize the boarded-up stores, but it all happily looked rather vibrant. I went into both the Downtown Development Office and the Chamber of Commerce looking for a bumper sticker that said Freehold. They were busy cancelling a parade and looked at me as if I were only visiting this planet, and totally unaware of the COVID-19 plague. My quest for a bumper sticker from Freehold remained unfulfilled. I thought of the plague as a historical occurrence from ages long past that no longer applied to us in the modern scientific age. If I still acted, up to that point, as if the kaleidoscope had not turned, getting back into the Pilot, recounting my adventure to Rhonda, cemented that the times indeed are not changing, but have changed.

We cruised ever so slowly the streets of Freehold, trying to absorb as much as possible. When we passed by the store Especially for You, Rhonda said she wanted to shop a bit. I parked across the street and waited. Returning from the shop with a print from Freehold, appropriately enough named *My Hometown*, she recounted the stories she had learned from the cashier—how Bruce gave a firetruck to the city—how Bruce and his family bring their folding chairs and watch the town's parade with everyone else—how Bruce is just like all of them despite being worth perhaps half a billion dollars. We took a picture of the Highway 9 sign and then drove to Asbury Park.

It was a cold and blustering day as the wind whipped up the waves. We parked across the street from the Stone Pony. It looked closed. Sitting in the SUV, we checked emails, and then watched the ocean for a minute or two. Crossing the road, we knocked on the door of that legendary musical establishment. A woman greeted us, and I asked if we could look about. She said, "Of course" and could not have been more hospitable. I wish United Methodist churches were as welcoming as the closed down Stone Pony.

Walking around taking photos, we drank in the Rock and Roll history with all the great acts who played there. Our tour guide explained who had signed this guitar and that guitar. We took a photo in front of the big Asbury Park sign that served as the cover of one of Springsteen's albums. I should have sent out that photo to friends with the words, "Greetings from you know where," but I was too busy listening to our guide tell us Springsteen stories. Like the lady in the Especially for You store, everyone has a Springsteen story except me, who had lived in Jersey for three years.

We had lunch at the Robinson Ale House with a magnificent view of the ocean. After lunch, walking down the board walk, I took pictures of Madam Marie's Fortune Telling Booth, and of Rhonda standing next to a lamp post. I figured it would not lead us to Narnia, as it had an Asbury Avenue Street sign attached to it. Stopping along the way looking in the windows of shops that were closed, we meandered down the board walk until we got to the Old Casino and Carousel House and then made our way back to the vehicle.

Climbing into the Pilot, I checked my emails and read the message from Bishop Paul Leeland of the Western North Carolina Conference. He called for the suspension of in-person worship for the next two weeks. I appreciated that the bishop had prioritized the health of his preachers and the laity over the financial needs of the institution. Reading some of the comments on the Conference Facebook page, it was clear that not everyone greeted his caring and thoughtful words warmly. One person responded with accusations that the bishop was in effect doing the devil's business by shutting down in-person worship. But dutiful to the bishop's decree, calling part of my pastoral team back in Kernersville, we mapped out plans for moving from a community that only worshipped in-person to a community that would for the short-term (so we thought) only worship by livestream.

Rhonda and I drove from Asbury Park to Wrightstown to have dinner with John. After picking him up, we made our way to the Texas Roadhouse in Hamilton Township. Talking about the Bishop suspending in-person worship for two weeks, we also discussed the snippets that we had heard on the radio and what we gathered from looking at CNN's website on the phone. The cancellations fell like a hard rain. After dinner, we went to a store to pick up some groceries, and we bought the last four pack of toilet paper. Whoever thought a day would come when TP would become a rare commodity? After taking John back to his apartment, we unloaded the groceries and the prized toilet tissue. Hugging him goodbye, we made plans for Friday evening.

When Rhonda and I got back to the hotel, we turned on the news. The reporting for Thursday evening was like an avalanche of bad news. The NCAA's March Madness tournament was cancelled. The NBA, the NHL, and the MLB postponed their season until a later unknown date. Broadway went dark. Hollywood shut down and Disney Land and Universal Studios announced they were doing the same. Tom Hanks and Rita Wilson were in Australia quarantined with the coronavirus. Airlines cancelled even more flights, and cruise lines were bringing ships to available ports. Americans traveling overseas were stranded, trying to find a way home.

The US was lagging other nations in developing testing kits for the virus. Somehow the nation that could put a man on the moon, invent the internet (with apologies to Al Gore), and countless other scientific marvels was suddenly getting clobbered in medical research and development. Europe was now an epicenter of the outbreak. Ireland was closing schools. Italy shut down the country with only grocery stores, pharmacies, and other essential businesses open. The DOW Jones plunged by over two thousand points, and the safety circuit breaker that prevents a massive selloff tripped for the second time in four days. The last time that the safety switch had been used was twenty-three years ago; this was the worst market day since 1987. The reporter stated that the experts do not know how long the pandemic would last. It could last weeks, maybe even months. The news anchor said that we are in uncharted territory.

Friday morning, drinking coffee in the room, watching the news, we wondered if another shoe was about to drop. After all, it was Friday the thirteenth and, after yesterday's cascade of events that were unimaginable a week before, anything now seemed possible. Gathering the items needed for the day, we made our way to the Pilot. Driving from the hotel to the Seminary library parking lot, where we left the SUV, we walked down Mercer Street heading toward downtown. Not far from the Princeton Battle Monument is the Albert Einstein bust on a granite pedestal. Carved into the granite is a quote from the Nobel Prize winning physicist: "Imagination is more important than knowledge. Knowledge is limited whereas imagination embraces the world." Though Einstein was referring to the importance of imagination and artistic thinking in the sciences, one is left to wonder in the current crisis of the church if part of the difficulty resides in our clinging to forms and patterns that need to be reimagined. United Methodist congregations have far too often resisted embracing reawakened imagination in favor of the status quo.

I am not sure why Einstein was on my mind that day. Perhaps, it was because the next day was his birthday. Back in my student days, one did not have to look very far to find an Einstein story. He had been no stranger to the Seminary. He and Professor Elmer Homrighausen worked together to help bring refugees from Nazi Germany to Princeton. Einstein also gave a lecture at the Seminary in 1939. I remembered hearing stories of how seminarians would be Christmas caroling in the neighborhood, and Einstein would come out and accompany them on a violin. Hugh Miller recounted that as a seminary student and a member of the Benham Eating Club, he had invited Einstein to attend the club's Christmas meal to celebrate the season and the approaching end of term.[1] Miller wrote that Einstein loved to talk. After dinner, they joined together in Christmas carols, and Einstein sang along with gusto. Plenty of seminarians, back in those days, had Einstein stories to tell.

Of course, there was also no shortage of Einstein stories floating around town. Stories of him getting on a bus struggling to make change, and the bus driver quipping to the other passengers, "He's bad at arithmetic."[2] It is far easier to believe that story of C.S. Lewis, than of Einstein. There were stories of him getting lost in town and forgetting how to get home. There were stories of children asking him for help with their math homework. They claimed the great scientist took time to instruct them in mathematics.[3]

In his book *An Anecdotal Memoir*, Charles Templeton recounted a similar story that his wife Connie shared with him.[4] She worked at the

1. Miller, "Christmas Past."

2. Mackin, "The Day Einstein Went Public."

3. See Edelstein, "Albert Einstein was a Princeton genius. And math tutor." With a quick Google search one can find more testimonies of former children who stated that Einstein helped them with their homework.

4. Charles Templeton was a famed Canadian evangelist, a friend and traveling companion of Billy Graham as they made their way and name as young bucks conducting revivals across North America and Europe. Templeton was said to have been a better

Chapin School teaching English and Music. Another teacher had a student who was having difficulties understanding the teacher's explanations of how to do multiplication and division. The frustrated teacher said, "Well, if you can't understand me, you'd better get Mr. Einstein to explain it to you."[5] According to Templeton, the child, who was a neighbor of the great scientist, did just that, and Einstein even signed her math homework. The school framed and hung it on a prominent wall.

Perhaps we devour stories of the absent-minded professor, for they somehow humanize and soften someone of such immense raw intellectual power. One of my favorite Einstein stories was told by Tom Long, who was my homiletics professor:

> The old-timers in Princeton, NJ love to tell the story of the time in the 1930s when a fashionable New York society matron drove to Princeton in her touring car. She pulled up to the entrance of the Princeton Inn. She stepped out of her car, fished around in her purse until she found a quarter, pressed it into the hand of the little man at the entrance of the hotel, saying, "Take my luggage in immediately." She then breezed regally into the hotel entrance, leaving the "little man" at the entrance of the hotel, who just happened to be Albert Einstein on the way to his office, looking quizzically at the quarter in his hand. As the story goes, eventually he shrugged his shoulders, picked up the luggage, and took it into the lobby. It was just a case of mistaken identity, misjudged appearances; it could happen to anyone. She took one look at the wild haired man in front of the hotel and assumed he was the bellhop, rather than the most distinguished scientist of our time.[6]

Princeton loves its most famous and revered citizen. Einstein was attached to Princeton enough to stay. He had plenty of offers from around the world. Oxford and numerous other universities wanted him in residence. Who would not want on their faculty the most significant scientific mind since the age of Galileo Galilei and Isaac Newton? And of all the places to live and with all the offers for teaching and research positions, he chose the

---

preacher than Graham. As time went by, however, Templeton started to struggle with theological questions that he could not answer, and thus he enrolled at Princeton Theological Seminary to study theology. After he left Princeton, those questions would eventually unravel his faith. He invited Graham to come to Princeton with him, but Billy, already the president of a Bible college, was worried how it would look.

5. Templeton, *An Anecdotal Memoir*, 77.

6. Long, email to the author (April 6, 2021).

Institute for Advanced Study and the town of Princeton. Einstein once said of the town, Princeton is "a wonderful little spot, a quaint and ceremonious village of puny demigods on stilts."[7]

Einstein moved to Princeton in 1933 but not as one unfamiliar with the town. He had made multiple trips there. In 1921, the University bestowed on him an Honorary Doctor of Science degree. By 1930, he was already spending part of the year at the Institute for Advanced Study. When he moved to Princeton permanently, he made his home at 112 Mercer Street until he died in 1955. His former house is close to the Seminary, and it was not uncommon, as a student, to see tourists with cameras around it, even though there was no plaque on the house or sign in the front yard that identified it as Einstein's former home.

When the Nazis came to power in 1933, the Jewish intelligentsia were in the crosshairs of their sights. Einstein, one of the most famous scientists in the world, was an identified target. Fortunately, he was traveling abroad when the Third Reich took control of Germany. Einstein's works were among those that were burned, and a magazine listed him as an enemy of the state, marking him as "not yet hanged," while putting a bounty on his head. His apartment in Berlin and his cottage in Caputh were ransacked, and the Nazis confiscated his sailboat and seized his financial assets. Yet, Einstein was one of the lucky ones, with a Nobel Prize and an international reputation. He could write his own ticket.

Millions of others did not have a magical ticket to escape the unfolding maelstrom that quickly turned into a global horrific nightmare. Not everyone could vacate Germany, nor did everyone want to leave the Fatherland. Back in 1979, my freshman year at Arkansas Tech University, in my dorm (Turner Hall) on the first floor, lived a college student who looked out of place. For the most part, we were teenagers and young men in their early twenties, though some were in the mid-twenties and were on the six- or seven-year plan of attaining their undergraduate degree. This resident was in his sixties. We shared rural or suburban Arkansas accents. His was a thick German accent, even though he had lived in America for many years.

One day, the aged student said that he had served in the German Army during the Second World War. With the arrogance of a seventeen-year-old, I asked, "How could you? How could you have served in the army for a monster like Hitler?" His answer stopped me in my tracks. He said, "Before Hitler, I had no shoes for my feet, and no potatoes for my stomach.

---

7. Hastings, "On March 14, all eyes in Princeton are on Einstein."

The German Army gave me both." I who had more than enough to eat and plenty of pairs of shoes for my feet, looked at the floor, lost for words.

So many years later, while strolling down Princeton's streets, I thought of my many blessings that far exceeds potatoes and shoes. Scripture teaches that blessings are accompanied with responsibilities. One of those responsibilities that accompany American citizenship, I believe, is to protect and preserve democracy from threats within and from without, and yet what have I done? Truth is, I have done very little except take it all for granted like a birthright rather than embracing the reality that it can disappear all too quickly. Democracy must be secured anew in every generation.

We looked through the shops on Palmer Square and took a few photos outside of the Yankee Tap Room and the Nassau Inn, where we had stayed during the Alumni Reunion two years prior. Remembering back to that time, the lectures were good, but two memories stand out. What I remember most of all is how much I missed my friends who are scattered across the country. Secondly, I reflected on how refreshing it was to have conversations about mission, evangelism, and how to lead our churches into becoming more like "the beloved community" without the rancor and divisiveness that inhabits the present United Methodist Church. My friends serve in denominations (The Presbyterian Church USA and the Lutheran Church ELCA) that had already navigated the storm of same-sex marriage and ordination. Their denominations chose to allow for space for congregations to make their own choices on how they handle such a critical pastoral care need. Yet, it needs to be noted that those denominations also lost a significant number of congregations and members due to their inclusive stance.

After snapping the photos in front of the Nassau Inn, Rhonda and I continued to browse and shop. While Rhonda looked at woolen clothing, I took photos of pictures in the Einstein Museum, which is in the back of the Landau store, a most inauspicious monument to the great man. Perhaps, that is fitting. Einstein did not want his house turned into a museum, nor his office at the Institute. He also wanted his ashes scattered at an undisclosed location. The Einstein Museum markets itself as the only permanent Albert Einstein exhibit in the United States.

I took a picture featuring Einstein on a sailboat and snapped a shot of his office with a chalkboard full of formulas that I did not comprehend. I took the photo mainly because his desk is as messy as mine. I captured another photo of Einstein playing a violin. I took that for my daughters

Laura and Emily who took violin lessons. I tapped the iPhone and got a picture of Einstein sitting on steps wearing fuzzy house slippers, and then I took a photo of a poster of Einstein with the words, "I want to know God's thoughts . . . the rest is details." As a practical theologian, I thought, "That would be nice." As I was about to leave the store, my attention was grabbed by one more poster. It too had a picture of Einstein with these words: "The world will not be destroyed by those who do evil, but by those who watch them without doing anything." Walking out onto the sidewalk, Einstein's words haunted my thoughts.

After lunch at Panera Bread, we crossed the road, walking back through the gates to the University. This stroll reminded me of another day, another walk, many years before. In the spring of 1986, I took a creative writing class. It met in the Creative Arts Building at 185 Nassau Street. I would pass Brooke Shields in the hallway. I do not remember having a crush on her as I was infatuated, at that time, with Vanna White. I liked how she turned the letters on *Wheel of Fortune*; I suspected she had a propensity for the written word. But Brooke's situation appeared to me as challenging. It must have been difficult to live in the celebrity fishbowl, but she handled it with grace. Not that I would ever have a clue to what she went through, but as the years passed, I began to understand the challenges that clergy and their families face living in another kind of fishbowl as the first family of the church.

After class one day, I bombarded the professor (Bill Henderson) with questions and he, who had a train to catch, invited me to walk with him. We traveled together until our paths diverged. He had thinning hair, and it blew in the wind. He wore a jacket that reminded me of a longshoreman. I appreciated that, as I routinely sported my Philips 66 all-weather service station jacket to classes and around town. The other outer apparel that I frequently wore was a long wool trench coat that was my father's. Some moths had properly aged it. For years, it had a button on it from the summer of 1982 backpacking Europe that said, *Atomkrieg, Nein Danke!* (Atomic War, No Thanks). I lost that one day in Firestone Library.

Henderson did not lack confidence. An outsider, he founded a press and became part of the literary landscape. Carrying the establishment attribute lightly, he was an intriguing teacher even if he dissed Ernest Hemingway. What did he say about him? Hemingway is okay if all you want to write about are football players and cheerleaders. I was offended on three counts. Along with Al Bundy, I possess no shame over those moments of gridiron combat. As the summer gave way to the fall under the stadium's lights, with the bleachers filled with cheering crowds, memories were made. Somewhere, out there, it is possible that a Subiaco Academy Trojan football exists with my signature on it. A boy I did not know asked for it. My one and only request for a sports memorabilia autograph! In addition, my Yamaha 650 was named Ernie in honor of my youthful literary hero whose paternal grandparents had attended, interestingly enough, that evangelical bastion, Wheaton College, whose most famous son was Billy Graham. The third offense I took that day is that I had dated cheerleaders and later would marry one. It is all so terribly Southern.

Hemingway, what was it about him that I found so appealing? No matter whether you care for him or not, every writer after him had to contend with him. But it was not just his written word. It was the image that he projected. In photos, he is smiling like a lottery winner, with confidence overflowing that the world will bend his way. Hemingway, the high priest of sucking the marrow out of life, the pope of the cult of experience, Mr. *Carpe Diem* himself, always seizing the day, had the world and, so it would seem, women falling at his feet. Perhaps that is why so many young men found in him an idol to embrace and emulate. From Paris to Pamplona to Havana, from the battlefields of Italy to Spain to France and Germany, Hemingway, in his quest for zest seemed bullet proof, just like I thought I was as a young man.

Of course, life is far more complicated than what is revealed in photographs. I suspect I have read *A Moveable Feast* far too many times. The beauty of his prose written by an old man looking backwards elicits romantic longing, a *Sehnsucht*, for a robust and full life that he once seemed to live before he became battered, bruised, concussion ridden, alcohol-ridden, and broken in so many places where he did not actually become stronger. The book did not capture the reality of his life during the Paris years, nor the heartache that I am sure the women in his life and their families endured. During those years, Hadley's marriage to Ernest ended when she learned of his affair with Pauline. I wonder what Pauline's parents, Paul and Mary Pfeiffer, back in Piggott, Arkansas, thought. Seizing the day can bring a tidal wave of grief to others.

Yet I remained an ardent fan of Hemingway's work, despite Henderson's objections. But I also enjoyed hearing Henderson's vignettes of his early years as a writer, and his stories of being a New York editor, and how in time, he started *The Pushcart Press*, borne out of the frustration with corporate publishing. If I remember right, he was either fired or about to be sacked by Doubleday. He gave us books from his press. The comment that he made that I never forgot is: if you want to be a very good writer, not a hack, not a verbal prostitute, then be prepared to be ignored for the rest of your life. He thought my fiction was over the top, very maudlin, and that my characters were too southern gothic. It did not take me long in that class to realize that I did not have the "right stuff" to be a novelist. Even though that was not a real ambition, a clarifying experience is always helpful to dispel daydreams. It is kind of like spending days deluding oneself that one could be Tom Brady, even though one is built like the Pillsbury Dough Boy. Henderson did give me some helpful advice when he told me to write what I know.

As we walked across campus, Henderson peppered me with questions as to why I wanted to attend seminary and enter the "God-business." I felt somewhat like an exhibit at the Zoo. It was a rambling conversation complete with comments about southern mountain dialects and Elizabethan English. Somehow, he worked in something that was meant to shock me. We probably were talking about Hemingway and the literary elevation of experience. Henderson had lived, and he knew there was emptiness at the bottom of that well. Hemingway knew it as well, but his larger-than-life personae with magazine covers demanded the perpetuation of that myth.

When we got to the intersection of University Place and Dickinson Street, Henderson asked me if I had read Tolstoy. I said, "Not much." What I wanted to tell him was that I thought Tolstoy's books were far too long. I prefer the novella. My attention span is lacking. How Maxwell Perkins ever waded through Thomas Wolfe's voluminous manuscripts, I do not know.[8] Henderson suggested I start consuming Tolstoy, for he saw in Tolstoy's spirituality something, I suspect, that he thought I needed. As we parted that day, he continued straight on past McCarter Theatre on his way to the Dinky. I do not remember if he were heading to New York City or Long Island.

Princeton was the kind of place where you could hear lectures by any number of writers and poets. It was the kind of place where you could have breakfast with Hans Küng.[9] Princeton was the kind of place where you could

---

8. See Berg, *Max Perkins* for a witness to Perkins's longsuffering work as an editor.

9. Hans Küng, (1928–2021) a Roman Catholic priest was a Professor of Ecumenical Theology at the University of Tübingen. He was stripped of his license to teach Roman Catholic theology by the Vatican when he rejected Papal Infallibility.

frequently run into Joyce Carol Oates in Firestone Library.[10] (I thought she had the eyes of a doe deer, not exactly skittish, but attentive to what was going on around her.) Princeton was the kind of place where you could take a short cut through the University campus and catch Eudora Welty receiving an Honorary Doctorate of Literature.[11] Princeton was the kind of place where there were more cultural opportunities than time afforded.

What of those opportunities would I now want to give back or have taken away? Would I want to cancel any of those memories, walking with Henderson, having conversations with world-class theologians, biblical scholars, church historians, and practical theologians? Would I want to forget about the trips to Cambridge to hang out at Harvard and hear Richard Reinhold Niebuhr lecture?[12] Or trips to Newport with Charlie Ryerson, a Buddha shaped, Scotch drinking Episcopalian who was a Comparative Religion scholar? Or spending time at Cintra Carter-Sander's house that I thought was a mansion?

Cintra was one of those generous and kind Princeton characters; an artist whose father, as a child, survived the sinking of the Titanic and who also had a relative that had been appointed to a diplomatic post in Portugal by President James Madison.[13] Cintra told great stories. She came from old money, and I believe, if I remember correctly, part of it derived from railroad stocks. She would have had even more resources if it had not been for one of her husbands who fancied himself a stockbroker. Just because one has excelled in one area does not make one an expert in all areas. Cintra also had a great way of correcting my course when I would wax political and become far too cynical. She would upbraid me with the comment, "Oh, you are far too young to sound like that."

Back then, ideas were as life-giving as the air we breathed. Of all the opportunities and experiences, I was gifted in those years, to which of them would I now want to return? Would I want to give back the evenings in the

10. Joyce Carol Oates is a Professor Emeritus of Creative Writing at Princeton University. A prolific author, she has won too many accolades and published far too many books to recount.

11. Eudora Welty, a daughter of Mississippi, was a master of the short story and a Pulitzer Prize winning author.

12. Richard Reinhold Niebuhr (1926–2017), a long-time member of Harvard Divinity School was a member of an American theological dynasty. His father H. Richard Niebuhr spent his career teaching theology at Yale University, and his uncle Reinhold Niebuhr taught at Union Theological Seminary in New York.

13. Obituary for Cintra Carter-Sander, *The East Hampton Star.*

Annex, the local watering hole, that advertised itself on its menus as the kind of place where you can share a drink with a mailman on one side of you and a world-class physicist on the other? Princeton establishments do get a bit woozy on their self-promotions. Or late nights lying out on the grass staring at the stars wondering what life will bring? Would I trade all of these to return home to Prairie View Ridge Mountain surrounded by the Ozark and the Ouachita mountains and have class on a laptop, and my only conversational partners are the cows that pass by my bedroom window? As I watched the students load up their cars, heading back to their homes, having their semesters gone virtual, being shortchanged of all the forthcoming rich experiences that they were to receive that would shape and be transformative, I grieved for their loss. What a raw deal they were being given!

Walking back to the Pilot, we drove to the hotel. While drinking a cup of coffee before leaving for Wrightstown, I remembered with gratitude my Princeton years. It is true that the Seminary had not prepared my class to face the long, painful decline of the church. Back in those days, our education led us to believe that society eagerly awaited our words as preachers and practical theologians, and large steeple churches beckoned. The future was so bright that we would need to wear shades.

After relaxing for a while, we made our way to Wrightstown picking up John and heading to Chili's in Trenton for dinner. Discussing all the recent events, we pondered what it all would mean. How quickly the world can change in a brief period. John talked about his hopes of finding another job and moving back to the South. After dinner we went shopping to get a few things that he needed. When we dropped him off at his apartment, we made plans for brunch in the morning. One last meal together before we headed back to North Carolina.

When we returned to the hotel, we made decaf coffee and watched the news. The shock began to wear off. We were now living in a "new normal" as we listened to the stories of the day. Trump, surrounded by CEO's, declared the coronavirus a national emergency. It was a mixed message event. A national crisis had been declared by the leader of the Free World. All the while no masks were worn, no social distancing observed, and the President shook the hands of the corporate leaders. The cases in the US now topped two thousand and, at least forty-nine deaths were attributed to it. Schools and churches were closing. The Boston Archdiocese suspended all in-person masses, and other churches across the country were following suit. Concerts, theme parks, other large public venues, such as the National

Zoo, and museums including the Smithsonian were shutting down. Grocery stores were in chaos with people standing in lines for hours to get into stores that were already depleted of necessities. Yet, Wall Street rallied by over two thousand points.

Chapter 7

TRAVELING SOUTH

ON SATURDAY, AFTER CHECKING out of the hotel, we drove to Wrightstown to pick up John. Wandering through the New Jersey countryside, we made our way to Mount Holly. It never ceases to amaze me how people whose only knowledge of New Jersey derived from flying in and out of Newark have such a limited and negative view of it. There is a reason why it is called the "Garden State" and, as we passed the horse farms and countryside, I pondered how pleasant it would be to live there.

After parking the Pilot, we crossed the street and opened the door to Kitchen 87. As we entered, we looked for an available table. The restaurant was packed, and the tables were so close together that one could easily grab a biscuit from a nearby neighbor. No one wore a mask. No temperatures were taken upon entering. Social distancing, obviously, was not, at that point, even part of the conversation. Six weeks after Trump had been notified that the coronavirus epidemic could be on par with the 1918 Influenza Pandemic, and we are all operating as if the major method of contracting this virus is from grabbing hold of contaminated doorknobs and then wiping one's nose or eyes.

The attentive, pleasant waitress had family in North Carolina. The food was excellent. We talked about the pandemic and last night's shopping excursion. The store shelves were sparse and not a roll of toilet paper to be found. We spoke hopeful words that the service stations along the way, in this age of imminent hoarding, would have enough gasoline to get us and other travelers to our destinations. After the meal, we took a few selfies outside the restaurant.

Heading back to Wrightstown, John talked again about how he wanted to move back South. Parking outside his apartment, we hugged our son goodbye. As I drove away, I reflected on the growth that I had seen in him since he had moved to New Jersey and was so proud of the man that he was becoming. At first, we listened to the Springsteen channel, our own version of an adieu to Jersey, a place that Rhonda and I obviously hold dear. We had met in Princeton and built a life together.

After we had been traveling awhile, Rhonda opened *Leaving Church* and began to read. Barbara Brown Taylor recounted the odyssey that the little Episcopal Church in the mountains of North Georgia went through when they called their first female priest. The congregation lost a third of their membership, but it was not long before others came to take their empty seats. The church grew so much they hired a second priest. When the mission congregation went solo, the associate pastor went with them, and thus Grace-Calvary hired another associate pastor. The congregation established the first church-related counseling center in town and opened a hospice office in the parish house. Sunday Services grew from two to three and then to four. Her reputation as a preacher grew in Georgia and beyond to the rest of the country.

I remember listening to Taylor preach at one of the national preaching conferences in the mid-1990s. Waiting in line with my copy of *The Preaching Life*, the preacher in front of me gushed on and on about how Taylor's writings had impacted her. Taylor stood there smiling, ever gracious. Not wanting to make a similar scene, I casually inquired if she would sign my book, which she did. In 1996, she was named by Baylor University as one of the twelve most effective preachers in the English-speaking world. Her star was not rising; it had already ascended, which would bring her privileges and options that few clergy enjoy.

As her fame as a pulpiteer increased, people came to check out what was going on in the quaint Episcopal Church that had suddenly become the talk of the region. The growth, of course, led to more obligations and responsibilities. Her day planner that once seemed useless now was full. Fatigue set in as she attempted to balance it all: more hospital visits, more nursing home residents and shut-ins to take the Eucharist to, more telephone calls, more church publications to oversee, and more publication deadlines for the steady stream of books that she produced. Then it happened. There were too many balls in the air. If she dropped one, she feared a parishioner would have a meltdown, being disappointed in her not meeting his or her needs. One of the vocational challenges for the clergy is that Jesus, a water-walker, miracle-worker, set a high standard and expectation about what leaders of the faith can indeed accomplish. One is guaranteed to face a long line of disappointed parishioners over the course of a ministerial career. The demands of ministry became an impediment for Taylor to experience God's presence.

As the congregation outgrew the size of the current facilities, conversations began about whether a building program was the next step or not. The church hired consultants to help them define and refine the vision. Of course, this now meant more meetings and increased anxiety in the congregation. Would the proposed construction project negatively impact the church's outreach? Would it hamper the congregation's budget for the ministries and maintenance of current facilities? During a congregational meeting, hotly debating whether to go forward with the proposed project or not, one man blurted out: "We are not going into debt to build you a preaching emporium."[1]

Churches are, by and large, homeostatic organizations and when change is introduced into the system, the preacher becomes an obvious lightning rod for the community's angst and anger. It is tempting when growth occurs to view it either as a sign of God's blessing or else a problem for the status quo. Amid the growth, expectations remain that the preacher will continue to hold hands and meet the needs, all the while the administrative responsibilities increase multiple times over. After all, Jesus had no difficulty feeding five thousand with five loaves and two fish. The implied question for the minister is, "So, what's your problem?"

On July 15, 2018, I preached my first sermon at Main Street UMC. Before moving to the church, I met with the then Senior Pastor Claude Kayler. Reviewing the challenges that he and the congregation faced, he provided me with a history of the congregation's plans to build a new building during the tenure of Jeff Patterson, the Senior Pastor before Claude. The church intended to construct a multipurpose building which would provide a place for youth and children to play basketball and would also have a space big enough so that one could have a church-wide meal. The current Fellowship Hall seats approximately a hundred and fifty, and parishioners dreamt of a space where they could accommodate if not the entire worship attendance

---

1. Taylor, *Leaving Church*, 100.

of around five hundred, then at least close to it. This was an intensely felt need since Main Street UMC, prior to the pandemic, had three Sunday morning worship services, and many parishioners did not and still do not know each other. The congregation had architectural plans drawn up, complete with a scale model and launched a capital campaign. The campaign generated a significant amount of money. However, it did not generate sufficient monies to move forward with the multi-purpose building.

During Claude's administration, the church realized that the expected cost of the proposed building had mushroomed to somewhere between seven and eight million dollars and that was too great a sum. Questions were also raised about whether Kernersville really needed another church with a gym. The vision changed instead to build a building that would tie together the existing three buildings of the Sanctuary, Chapel, and Education. The cost of the proposed new construction was approximately four million. Before any Church or Charge Conference could be held to launch a capital campaign or to select a contractor, Claude announced that he was leaving at the end of his fourth year. His announcement came as an abrupt disruption in the minds of those who bought in to building the proposed building and let loose fears, among a few, that somehow the process might be derailed under the new unknown Senior Pastor.

Claude had already weathered in his time as Main Street's Senior Pastor tremendous staff conflict. He had also led the congregation through the process of changing the vision from one expected outcome in new construction to something entirely different. Claude decided that he needed a break from pastoring congregations. He took a sabbatical and founded a coaching and consulting business. Prior to the pandemic, too many talented clergy were leaving local church ministry. One wonders, what will be the impact of the pandemic upon clergy tenures in congregations and the impact on the number of pastors exiting from the local church altogether?

In June of 2021, Claude retired from active ministry in the conference. After Annual Conference, I called him and asked, "You are only 58. Why are you retiring?" He said, "Mike, with the impending division of the denomination and possibly of the annual conference, I wanted to retire from the same annual conference and the same denomination that my father had served." Tragically, on July 16 of that same year, Claude, an avid cyclist, was killed in an accident.

On November 18, 2018, I presided over a special Church Conference to vote on proceeding with the building project and launching a Capital

Campaign. Prior to this Church Conference, there had already been ex-pressions of concern, just like Grace-Calvary Episcopal, on the impact the proposed new construction would have on the church budget, mission giv-ing, maintenance of existing buildings, program ministries, and staffing. I also harbored many of those same concerns.

In addition, I wondered about the United Methodist Church's (in the United States) more than half century of membership decline that went from more than eleven million members in 1968 to now less than six and a half million. I also pondered how that trajectory would impact Main Street UMC. With the possibility of *The Protocol of Reconciliation and Grace through Separation* passing at the next General Conference, one could not help but be concerned about how the denominational split would affect the congregation. How many of the far right and the far left would exit out the front and back doors of the church? Furthermore, is there a point when the denomination's brand name becomes problematic for the local church? Lovett Weems in 2011, who at that time was Director of the Lewis Center for Church Leadership at Wesley Theological Seminary, predicted a com-ing death tsunami for the United Methodist Church.[2] When I preached on Sundays, I could not help but notice the graying of the congregation. Who will be here in fifteen years for the ceremony of burning the note?

Before we voted on the eighteenth of November, there was significant discussion about whether this was the right course of action or not. Some still held to the original vision of the multi-purpose building and felt that the intent of that should not be changed. The congregation needs to follow through with what it started, they contended. A comment was made that what is now, in fact, being proposed to be built is simply a glorified hallway that does not solve the problem of a needed space for youth and children in which to play, nor does it satisfy the expressed desire to be able to seat a significant number of the congregation for a sit-down meal. Different members of the Building Committee responded to each of these concerns, and after more discussion ensued, a motion was put forth to move forward with the building plans and the Capital Campaign.

An amendment was made to the original motion that 5 percent of the monies raised in the Capital Campaign would go to missions. The amend-ment passed. The new motion covering the Capital Campaign, moving for-ward with the building project, and the monies for mission passed as well. I was inspired by the confidence of the laity that the congregation could

2. Weems, *Focus*, 7, 8.

indeed weather all the storms facing the church in America and not only weather them, but flourish in the midst of them. We launched the Capital Campaign in January of 2019.

On August 11, 2019, I presided over a Church Conference. The primary purpose of the meeting was to select a contractor and approve the bid for the building project. We considered the bids from four different contractors and then a motion was made to accept one of them. The motion also stated that the cost of the proposed new Connections Building would not exceed 3.95 million. The motion also authorized the congregation to borrow up to two million dollars. The motion passed. On September 15, 2019, we broke ground.

After the parishioners of Grace-Calvary Episcopal Church had left one of the meetings, discussing whether to move forward with a building project or not, Barbara Brown Taylor walked around the room reading the break-out groups newsprint sheets that were taped to the wall. One comment was repeated on three different sheets: "Wait until Barbara leaves to decide this."[3] That is how she learned that her time there was drawing near. As she became more and more fatigued by the work, her grief increased, her tears flowed, and her resentments grew. She wrote, "Drawn to marry the Divine Presence, I had ended up estranged."[4] It is ironic, though not surprising, in this age of mainline decline, that Grace-Calvary's growth in worship attendance and membership ushered in challenges that would lead to Taylor finding the exit door.

As Rhonda read, I thought about what my friend Tom Gibson once told me. Gibson, a retired United Methodist pastor, led several congregations through significant building projects. He asked me one day, "You do know that the great majority of pastors have to leave their churches after a building project is completed, don't you?" "Thanks," I replied. "That's just what I needed to hear. Build a building and, along the way, climb Golgotha." Tom laughed and said, "Just wanted to cast a little sunshine your way."

I also pondered all the steps that we have taken to get us where are, half-way through building an almost four-million-dollar new construction, and yet tomorrow, in our already existing multi-million-dollar campus, not a single congregant will be allowed into the sanctuary, only the staff and pastors. This is just too surreal to contemplate, I thought. Needing a jolt of caffeine, we took the next offramp.

3. Taylor, *Leaving Church*, 100.
4. Taylor, *Leaving Church*, 102.

❊   ❊   ❊   ❊   ❊

As I merged the Pilot again onto the Interstate, Rhonda continued to read. During Barbara Brown Taylor's time as Rector of Grace-Calvary, the complicated issue of human sexuality came to the forefront of the Episcopalian denomination. Mandatory meetings were required of each parish church. For many years, the Episcopal Church, like so many other institutions in America, functioned under a modified version of "Don't Ask; Don't Tell." The denomination gladly received the giftedness and ministries of the gay and lesbian clergy and laity but refused to publicly acknowledge them with what I was taught as a child were the sacraments of ordination and marriage.

As Taylor presided over the required meetings in her church, she feigned neutrality.[5] As is so often the case, the conversations became increasingly bitter as each side appealed to the Scriptures to justify their arguments for either inclusion or exclusion. The Holy Scriptures, the source of God's eternal life-giving Word, can be quickly transformed into blunt instruments of warfare. The doctrinal differences impacted the quality of relationships among the parishioners. The conflict also took its toll upon Taylor's soul. She wrote, "Once I had begun crying on a regular basis, I realized just how little interest I had in defending Christian beliefs."[6] Taylor also took note of how the power struggle in the Episcopal Church affected those who were culturally left, "the poets began drifting away from churches as the jurists grew louder and more insistent."[7] The poets drifted away as the legalists became entrenched. That almost sounds like it could be an ending to the last chapter of the Gospel story before the Resurrection. Denominations need no other canary in the coal mine than the poets are exiting the church.

The conflict in the local church over whether to build or not, and the conflict in the denomination over whether to include or exclude certain people from ordination and marriage, along with all of the other demands of ministry, eventually wore down Taylor's soul, spirit, and attitude so much so that she stopped answering the phone on her days off. She also began to shut down in worship, and the parts of the liturgy that had once been lifegiving now presented questions that she struggled to answer. She who

5. Taylor, *Leaving Church*, 106.

6. Taylor, *Leaving Church*, 109.

7. Taylor, *Leaving Church*, 111.

formerly relished wearing a collar began to ask, "What else can I do for a living?" Open a hardware store? A bookstore? Just what was she qualified to do apart from the work of the clergy?

One afternoon, sitting at her desk, sorting through the mail, the phone rang. She answered. It was the president of a nearby school, Piedmont College. He said that the Board of Trustees recently established a new Chair in Religion and Philosophy, and they would like to consider her as a candidate for this position. She replied that she needed time to think about it. The next day, she returned his call and answered in the affirmative. As the college conducted a search, she spoke with her bishop and others, letting them know of this new possibility. The day finally arrived when the president called her and offered her the job. This time she did not need any time to think about it. She jumped at the chance. The following day, she notified the members of the vestry, and she also called the selected members of the church that she wanted to hear the news from her and not second or third-handed.

As Rhonda read, I listened to Taylor's preparations for concluding her ministry at the church. She had come to it in 1992 and then resigned her position in 1997. She was now ready for what was behind door number whatever. I listened as Rhonda read about the pool party and how Taylor let down her guard and enjoyed being with her people, no longer feeling separated by the collar. As she found herself in the pool with all the others, it was a newfound baptism of sorts.

Taylor's church-wide farewell event was held toward the end of September. She went to Grace-Calvary with the intention of giving that congregation at least a decade worth of her service, but after five and a half years, she realized that she was done. As she said, "My quest to serve God in the church had exhausted my spiritual savings."[8] Her duties at Piedmont College, as the Harry R. Putnam Professor of Religion, would not begin until January of 1998. She now had three months to decompress, breathe, and prepare for classes.

With Taylor's church duties in her rear-view mirror, she had, in front of her, for the interim between what was and what would be—time. Time to discover why God created a sabbath for humanity. Reflecting, she took note of how while working in God's vineyard, she rarely, truly observed the sabbath. Preachers are better at instructing than they are heeding the divine

8. Taylor, *Leaving Church*, 127.

mandate. There was always a sermon to tinker with, new talks to construct, phone calls to make, visits to do, and a wedding rehearsal to attend.

One of my friends, a second-career Presbyterian pastor, was jubilant that her two adult children were coming to see them for Christmas. After two or three days into the visit, they turned to their mom and said, "Thank you." She asked, "For what?" They replied, "For not going into the ministry until after we had left home." She was stunned. Then one of them said, "Since we have been here, you and dad have talked nonstop about the church." Even for people who are trained in the art of boundaries, the church has a way of enveloping those who labor in God's vineyard.

That first Sunday after leaving Grace-Calvary, Taylor chose not to spend it in her old church or in one of the nearby congregations. The cathedral was her front porch, reading the prayer book, listening to the birds sing, and basking in God's creation. There were no intrusive questions on that porch. No one demanded anything of her, wanting to know why she had made the decision that she made—no one else to look after or care for—just time to rediscover a sense of awe. In her mind, she framed an apology to all those parishioners through the years who approached her with excuses on why they skipped church last Sunday. We preachers have heard it all: the weather was too inviting, the fish were biting, the greens called out for eighteen holes, the jet ski just got back from the shop, and the mountain home, lake house, or beach house demands attention. Too often, we preachers project our own version of institutional loyalty upon parishioners: Got to keep them coming, got to keep the numbers up, seats in the pews, and checks in the offering plate.

What Taylor also discovered when she removed her collar is that she was now no longer identified as the holiest person in the room. She learned, by not wearing it that she also lost some of the deference that had been accorded her by strangers. When she did attend church, she no longer sat in the prominent chair, no longer presiding, no longer in charge. Changes, they come into our lives, whether invited or not. When they burst their way in, what we so often fail to realize are all the things that we took for granted, which, in fact, made significant imprints on our lives and souls. Taylor had lost her institutional power and role. She missed the baptisms, the funerals, the pastoral visits, the preaching, and most of all the breaking of the bread, elevating the cup, and leading her people into a two-thousand-year-old drama that has shaped and formed not only her parishioners, but followers of Christ through the ages, all the way back to that first Maundy Thursday, that Mandate Thursday of so long ago.

By losing her institutional power, she had gained tenderness toward other clergy, toward parishioners, and toward herself. She also had received a taste of spiritual poverty. The third thing that accompanied the loss of power was that she felt that her priesthood emptied into the world. She remembered what she always knew, that the "church is not a stopping place but a starting place for discerning God's presence in this world."[9]

Released from the burden of running the institution, Taylor became more intentional, living her faith fully. By no longer having to defend the faith, she had the opportunity to revisit the faith. What she discerned is that what she once held as essential now no longer remained in the center. Having spent so many decades in the edifice that Mother Church created, Taylor ventured off the safe grounds exploring the wilderness, seeking a larger world than the one that she previously had inhabited. Even as she began to experience the loss of Mother Church, she gained, a new attachment, the Holy Spirit.

Rhonda had been reading most of the day. We had come to the end of Chapter Fourteen. Needing a break, we turned on the radio and listened to Country Music the rest of the way home. Our fears over a shortage of gasoline proved unfounded. Pulling the Pilot into the garage, it was night. Leaving the luggage in the car until morning, we walked into the kitchen, grateful to be home. Still wired from the drive, we made some decaf coffee and watched the news to catch the stories that we had missed while on the trip.

The news was more of the same. New travel restrictions were announced for the UK and Ireland. France, Spain, and Israel are shutting down, and other nations are following suit. Hospitals are rationing supplies, and a fear exists that there will not be enough respiratory ventilators and not enough Intensive Care Unit beds across the nation to handle the impending storm. Nursing homes are now closed to visitors. Businesses are attempting to boost supplies to get the consumers what they need as the store shelves continue to be emptied. There are long lines across the country at coronavirus testing sites. Major retailers dealing with non-necessity items are closing their stores. Sunday in-person services are cancelled from coast to coast. Governor Roy Cooper of North Carolina announced that all schools are ordered closed. Trump had another press briefing. Everyone

9. Taylor, *Leaving Church*, 165.

had to have their temperatures taken before entering the press room, but no one wore a mask and no social distancing.

Just five days before, we had set out on our trip to visit our son. In those few days, the world had changed in ways that we never imagined.

Chapter 8

SHUTTING DOWN

SUNDAY MORNING, RHONDA AND I drank coffee and talked about how grateful we were that we made the trip to see our son and wondering how long it would be before we could make another trip. The news played in the background with its steady bombardments of stories that landed on our consciousness like explosions that once sounded far away but are now, with each blast, coming closer.

While waiting for the 9 am Livestream Service, my mind drifted back three decades. Watching TV Church is not something that we have done as a couple since we lived on Central Campus at Duke University. In those days, I worked Lock-Out and shared those duties with another graduate student. Every other weekend, one of us took call from Friday evening until Monday morning, being available for students who misplaced their apartment key. The other glorious responsibility entailed plunging clogged toilets. Thus, every other Sunday, you could find Rhonda and me attending church in our apartment via Duke TV being fed by the preaching of Will Willimon.

Now here we were, all these many years later, attending church again in our living room while drinking coffee. I asked Al Ward a couple of months prior to the pandemic to preach on March 15 and though I had no clue to an upcoming storm, it was a fortuitous choice. To say that Al has coins of credibility with the congregation is attuned to commenting that the ocean is wet. Al served on the church's ministry staff approximately five decades before when he was an undergraduate at High Point University. Years later, he returned as the Senior Pastor and served with distinction for five years before he was named a District Superintendent. Some years after that, he came back to serve as one of the Ministers of Visitation. Al gave a wonderful sermon grounded in the ever-abiding presence, hope, and love of God.

I struggle to fathom how the churches weathered the pandemic of 1918 and 1919 without the aid of technology. Even with this great asset, I was concerned about how long the storm would last and what would its effects be on the church's budget and capital campaign. Few people enter into the ministry to serve as institutionalist but, as the years pass, one takes note of just how much mental energy is given over to pondering and preserving structural concerns.

Late that Sunday afternoon, I went to the church office to collect my mail and messages. No one was in the building. Standing at my office window, looking out at the construction equipment and the torn-up grounds, I thought again about Saturday's ruminations. We are building a brand-new Connections Building, and parishioners are not allowed in the existing buildings: no Sunday School classes, no confirmation meetings, no choir rehearsals, and no spotting the preacher run from the 8:30 a.m. service in the sanctuary to the 8:45 a.m. Jubilee service in the Chapel.

Today, there were just two services: 9 a.m. and 11 a.m. The only people allowed in the facility were the pastors and staff needed to conduct the livestream service. From outward appearances, it looked like the church was closed, but what we were learning on a deeper level than before is what we already knew; the church is not a building. The church is the people of God drawn together to worship and to serve. On that first pandemic Sunday, we gathered virtually as a community.

On March 1, we broke bread, shared the cup, patted each other on the backs, shook hands, sang loudly, and worshipped together. On March 8, still patting each other on the backs, we did not shake hands. We sang and worshipped together, and we packed out the Fellowship Hall. On March 15, everyone except for the ministry team stayed home to sing, worship, and pray. The upside is one can now sit in a bathrobe, sporting fluffy bedroom slippers like the kind that Albert Einstein wore, drinking coffee, and making loud human noises without fear all the while the pastor preaches.

On Tuesday, we gathered for our usual set of morning meetings. We did not meet in the good size Sunday School classroom where we traditionally met, but instead in the larger space of the church parlor. We did our best to socially distance from one another. It was St. Paddy's Day, no parades in Dublin, or Manhattan. I thought of my dad that morning, as I do every St. Patrick's Day. It was one of his favorite holidays. I guess it was the green beer that captured his imagination, though one would have thought that his favorite feast day would have been St. Boniface's Day. Of course, as they say, "On St. Paddy's Day, everyone is Irish." Dad has been gone forty-seven years, but he still abides in my memory and in the church universal.

As a staff, we worked through the upcoming ministries that we were cancelling and wondered in what other ways could we meet those needs. We discussed moving as many ministries as we could to Zoom and Facebook platforms. I had never heard of Zoom until that day. We all wondered how long this pandemic would last. The bishop suspended in-person worship for two weeks, but we had our doubts that we would be back in the sanctuary before Easter.

Easter Sunday and an empty sanctuary, how does any of this make sense? Sure, we proclaim an empty tomb, but we expect to do that in a crowded sanctuary where everyone is dressed in their finest, and the choir, who has been dutifully preparing for months, belts out Handel's Hallelujah Chorus as the sound waves inundate the congregation. On Saturday, Governor Cooper issued an order for schools to close for in-person classes. On Ireland's patron's saint day, he ordered restaurants and bars to close for in-person dining.

We spent a lot of time in worship planning reflecting on how virtual worship changes how we lead worship. Now we are no longer looking out at all the faces we know so well: the tender faces of those who support and encourage—of those who frequently offer constructive criticisms—of those who are grieving—of those who are struggling through a divorce—of the ones who just got news that their job has been downsized or outsourced—of those whose families are torn apart by addictions, and to the hungry faces of those searching for meaning. Instead of beholding those faces we focused instead on the camera. Princeton Theological Seminary had not prepared me to be a TV evangelist. After worship planning, normally a group of us would go out to lunch at one of the Kernersville restaurants, but not today. We were just beginning to see how the pandemic would change the many ways we functioned that we took for granted.

On March 18, the announcement came that the General Conference meeting scheduled for May 5–15 was postponed. Though the postponement created disappointment from both the left and the right side of the denomination, it also provided relief for others. With the pandemic crashing down upon us and with the winds blowing from every which direction, the energies needed to be exerted, at that moment, were finding an answer to these questions: how does the local church navigate and weather the storm without capsizing? How does the church faithfully live into the mandate that Christ gave in the Great Commission? Jesus said,

> Go out and train everyone you meet, far and near, in this way of life, marking them by baptism in the threefold name: Father, Son, and Holy Spirit. Then instruct them in the practice of all I have commanded you.[1]

Some of my friends in the Wesleyan Covenant Association were afraid that an opportunity to leave the denomination taking local churches, Annual Conferences, and twenty-five million dollars might be missed if this storm lingered too long. I did not share that concern but not for the reasons you might suspect. The encampments were too entrenched and after more than a half century of arguing neither side had been able to decisively win the day. Due to the paralysis, I remained skeptical that the Protocol could exit General Conference anywhere close to the position it occupied at the beginning of GC. Would holding the denomination together with bailing wire and duct tape be preferred to division? I remained undecided and puzzled. What is clear is that the denomination will continue to lose evangelical megachurches to independent status.

Sitting in my office on that Wednesday, I was not frantically preparing for that evening study on the Gospel of Matthew. The church office sounded different that day. No parishioners dropped by for a visit. Everything seemed somewhat like a snow day except that the ground was not frozen, but time seemed to be, and if not frozen, at least suspended. If not frozen, and if not suspended, then time felt like one of those melting clocks in a Salvador Dali painting. Was time frozen or was time melting? I do not know, but everything seemed out of synch. No waiting for Rhonda to arrive from work in Statesville to walk over together for the Wednesday night Fellowship dinner. That was cancelled as well as almost everything else, except the Oasis Service that was livestreamed. Of course, no congregation was present. Working virtually from home that day, Rhonda watched the service by casting it from her iPhone to the TV.

---

1. Matthew 28:19b, 20a (*The Message*, 2339).

On March 19, the Main Street Book Club was scheduled to discuss *Leaving Church*. We postponed that conversation until April 23. Sitting in my office, I opened Taylor's book and began to read the last few chapters. In the space between the time that had been defined by serving as the Rector of Grace-Calvary Episcopal Church to the space that will be when she becomes the new Professor of Religion at Piedmont College, she prepared for her upcoming lectures. As the only professor in the religion department, she would teach Introduction courses to World Religions, the Bible, Christian Theology, and other more specialized courses. Her calendar had changed from following the liturgical seasons of Advent, Christmas, Epiphany, Lent, Easter, Pentecost, and Ordinary Time to the academic calendar of Fall and Spring Semesters. She took note of what she had lost: liturgical language, vestments, the collar, clerical status, and she also reflected upon what she had gained: a new freedom to love God, neighbor, and to accept herself in the midst of all of the changes taking place. Though vocationally she left the local church, she did not leave the church universal, nor did it leave her.

Do not let Taylor fool you with the title of her book; her vocation remains. She simply switched one pulpit for another. Like Graham Greene's whiskey priest, despite our failings, shortcomings, disillusionments, and sometimes loss of faith in organized religion, the call remains.[2] Like Isaiah, the preacher is the one with unclean lips living in a land of unclean lips.[3] The burning coal taken from the altar in the Lord's Temple and placed upon the preacher's lips burn deep into the soul leaving its mark, setting her or him apart.[4]

Like Jacob who crossed the ford of Jabbok and spent the darkness wrestling with a man that Hosea identified as an angel, the preacher wrestles with and is marked by Otherness.[5] Later, Barbara Brown Taylor would write another book about finding God in the dark.[6] Jacob named that place Penuel. Did he name it that for that is where he saw the face of God? Or is it for facing God, striving, and struggling with one's maker or at least one's maker's representative? Whatever it was and is, Jacob left that place and walked the rest of his days with a limp.

---

2. See Greene, *The Power and the Glory*.

3. Isaiah 6:5.

4. Isaiah 6:6–8.

5. See Genesis 32:22–32 and Hosea 12:4.

6. See Taylor, *Learning to Walk in the Dark*.

I have heard parishioners say that they would like to encounter an angel. I suspect it is because they have been watching too many reruns of shows starring Michael Landon and Roma Downey. There is a reason why, repeatedly, it is recorded in the Scriptures that an angel's first words upon meeting a human is, "Do not be afraid!"[7] There is certainly good reason for that. Some people after being touched by the noumena spend the rest of their days as the walking wounded. Once one has been touched, one is marked, and it does not matter whether the ministry is conducted in a congregation, a hospital room, a university lecture hall, or in the saloon down the street, the preacher will preach, the prophet will proclaim and denounce, the scribe will write, and the pastor will heal. The work of God continues, sometimes I believe, most profoundly, outside of the walls of the church building.

In this moment of time, as I write these words, this is where God has placed me, in Kernersville, North Carolina, in a congregation called Main Street, in the midst of a pandemic. I never dreamed in my youth that I would one day live in North Carolina. My dream back then was to somehow make it back to my birth state of California. Yet, there is mystery in living this life.

On March 22, I preached on John 9:1–12. The sermon title was "Who is to Blame?" It too is a familiar passage to most congregations. Any pericope dealing with theodicy is going to be hit upon by American preachers as they navigate the heresy of the prosperity gospel and the entitlement of American exceptionalism. The lectionary passage for that Sunday was John 9:1–41, but I chose to focus on just the first twelve verses.

It is a familiar question, isn't it? The disciples saw a man born blind, and asked, "Rabbi, who sinned, this man or his parents, that he was born blind?"[8] It would be easy, at this point, to throw stones at the disciples for being insensitive. The truth is, we all struggle with questions of theodicy. We all, in one way or another, ask those questions summed up in Rabbi Kushner's book, *When Bad Things Happen to Good People*.

When some misfortune befalls, people often want to blame others. If someone is homeless, you can hear a callous comment by a bystander about how it must be the street person's fault. You will hear people say, "Well, if they would just pull themselves up by their bootstraps," as if life is that simple. J. Seward Johnson Jr. had a plethora of options available to him that the

---

7. Some examples are Luke 1:13, 1:30, 2:10,

8. John 9:2 (NRSV).

denizens of my hometown do not. There are any number of conditions out of an individual's control that could render someone homeless. If someone gets cancer, you can hear people inquire, "Well, did they smoke?" Or "Did they live next to a Christmas tree farm where the grower illegally imported his or her pesticides from Mexico?" Or "Is there a history of cancer in the family?" It has got to be someone's fault. There must be some reason, some hidden knowledge, that we can glean so that this circumstance does not befall us. Somehow doing this verbal gymnastic inquiry helps people soften or ignore the hard truth that life is dangerous and has always been so. This is a fallen world and earthquakes, tornados, hurricanes, viruses, illnesses, and pestilence happen regardless of whether we are rich or poor, Caucasian or Samoan, American or Haitian, theist or atheist, Christian or Muslim.

When we think about the man in John's Gospel who was born blind, one imagines that he had enough trouble in his life, surviving in a world without any social safety nets, no Social Security, no Judean Disability Act. All he had was himself and some family. He did not need the judgment that was coming from the disciples. In the midst of these indignities, we see grace step in, like water falling on a parched desert. We see words of hope, like the winter snow starting to melt in a frozen land called Narnia. Jesus said, "Neither this man nor his parents sinned; he was born blind so that God's works might be revealed in him."[9] You see the change in the text.

The man born blind is no longer a man of sorrow, broken down, blinded by someone's mysterious sin. He is an instrument given to you, so that the blinders on your eyes can be removed. He is an instrument of God's power, which liberates you from the captivity of your own judgment and condemnation. He is an instrument of God's grace so that the scales will fall from your eyes, and you will behold the power of God's love. The blind man gains his sight, and the disciples and you and I learn to see through Jesus's eyes. We learn not to heap our bad theology upon those wounded. We learn not to dump our judgment and implied condemnation upon those who are hurting. How often have we heard the trite expression on a preacher's lips of "Love the sinner and hate the sin?" Those who struggle with whatever the preacher has elevated do not feel that so-called love. They feel isolated and judged. Contrast that clichéd preacher with Jesus who unburdens and releases the man from society's condemnation and isolation.

I shared with them that last week, Rhonda and I were in New Jersey visiting our son. One night, while watching the news, we heard an interview

9. John 9:3 (NRSV).

with a restaurant owner in a nearby city. This was before the government ordered shutdown of dining in restaurants. He was losing his livelihood because he was a Chinese American. People were uttering despicable words to individuals of Asian descent on the streets as if somehow it was their fault that the coronavirus came to our lands. When I heard that on the news, the first thing I thought was, "These people are forgetting who they are and whose they are." Of course, the other option is that it was not as much a case of forgetting as it was that no one ever shared with them the story of Jesus, and they live as strangers to divine love. Perhaps, they do not know that everyone is a child of God and should be accorded that respect and dignity. What is also true, my atheistic friends like to remind me, is that the institutional church fails to treat many with the worth that they too deserve as God's children.

This storm, this pandemic, that has seemingly come out of nowhere taps into our wells of anger and fear that we all carry. People are losing their jobs, their life savings, and high school seniors are losing their final season of which they worked so diligently to prepare for. People have lost mobility. Long anticipated trips to relatives in foreign lands have been cancelled. Most sobering, people have lost loved ones: so many dreams deferred, so many broken hearts.

In these very difficult days, let us remember the story that when Jesus and the disciples were out on the Sea of Galilee and a ferocious storm arose that frightened these professional fishermen, Jesus was in the boat with the disciples. He is also with us in this storm and calls us to remain faithful to who we are called to be despite our fears and anxieties.

Today's Scripture passage challenges us. We have a choice. When we see someone suffering, let us not ask, "What did you do to have misfortune visited upon you?" We live in a dangerous world, and tragedies and sufferings are a part of the fabric of this world. When someone has life pressing down upon them, instead of giving to them bad theology, let us reach out asking, "How can we help? How can we love you through this tough time?"

We have a choice in all of this. We can be agents of grace or agents of judgment. We can be encouragers or discouragers. We can be positive toward others, or we can be negative. The power is given to each one of us to choose. My prayer is that we will all become like Barnabas.[10] As we navigate this storm, let us commit to be sons and daughters of encouragement, reaching out to others, speaking uplifting words, giving assistance,

---

10. Acts 4:36. Barnabas means "son of encouragement."

and supporting one another. Let us pay attention to the guidelines from the Center for Disease Control and follow the recommendations that are given to us. Let us be partners in this war against the Coronavirus. Amidst this torrent, let us not forget who we are and whose we are.

I concluded the sermon with a story that James Michener shared in his autobiography *The World is My Home*. Michener was one of America's most prolific authors. He died in 1997. He wrote more than forty books, novels such as *Alaska, Caravans, Tales of the South Pacific, Texas* etc. He was known for writing stories that covered many generations, making a point to do extensive genealogical work on his characters, which is intriguing given his own personal circumstances. Michener never knew the identity of his birth parents or whether a birth certificate existed for him. He was raised by a widow woman named Mabel Michener who took in orphaned children for which she received a meager amount. Mabel's husband died young leaving her with a son Robert to raise and little financial means by which to do it. Though Michener extolled his adopted mother, the extended family treated him cruelly.

When the Michener aunts would visit, they would lavish Robert with bags of goodies, and then say to James, "You're not a Michener. You don't deserve any."[11] Though he idolized Robert, who Michener considered his older brother, he felt that his aunts turned Robert against him for when Robert moved away, he refused to have any contact with James for the next sixty years. As Michener made his way in life as a writer and as his fame and accomplishments grew, he started to receive mean-spirited anonymous letters ridiculing him for using a name that the letter writer said he had not right to use. The anonymous writer would sign his letters, "A real Michener."[12]

The letters continued through the years. After Michener received the Pulitzer Prize, the anonymous relative exploded in his venom, "Who in hell do you think you are, trying to be better than you are?"[13] After President Gerald Ford in 1976 bestowed upon him the highest national civilian honor (The Presidential Medal of Freedom), the toxic letters came with their haunting refrain, "Still using a name that isn't yours. Still a fraud. Still trying to be better than you are."[14] Michener said those words burned into his

11. Michener, *The World is My Home*, 483.
12. Michener, *The World is My Home*, 484.
13. Michener, *The World is My Home*, 485.
14. Michener, *The World is My Home*, 486.

heart, challenging him to rise above it. He acknowledged, "He was right on all of his accusations."[15] Michener confided, "I have spent my life trying to be better than I was, and am brother to all who have the same aspirations."[16]

As the storm rages, as the wind blows, and as the ground shakes, let us always remember who we are and whose we are. We are the sons and daughters of encouragement. We are the ambassadors of God's amazing grace and love.

I preached that sermon to an almost empty room. No parishioners were there, only the pastors and the staff needed for the livestream. It seemed strange to preach to vacant pews in a room that can hold somewhere between 750 to 900 people depending upon who you ask and whether the Fire Marshall is present or not. After I gave the Benediction, and after the postlude finished, we waited for the sign to be given that we were no longer on the air. As a team, we talked for a few minutes and then scattered in different directions, heading home. There were no hands to shake, and no hugs to be given. The world had changed, and we were coming to terms with it.

Sunday evening, sitting at home, I started posting the pictures from the trip to Princeton, Freehold, and Asbury Park. What I should have done is noted that the pictures were taken the week before. They showed up on Facebook as if they were happening in that moment. I began my posting-a-thon with the pictures taken following in the footsteps of the Boss: pictures of the "Welcome to Freehold, New Jersey" sign that hangs in the Downtown Development office, of Rhonda and me in front of the St. Rose of Lima Catholic Church, of me alone in front of Bruce's childhood home, of the Freehold High School, of a Highway 9 sign, of the Stone Pony, and of the Asbury Park boardwalk. As I posted, people started sharing their own Springsteen stories. Then came the comments that I should have expected but my surprise revealed just how far I had to travel to acclimatize to this new normal. Friends out of concern chided me and said, "Get home now. Shelter and be safe. This is no time for a sight-seeing trip; get back to North Carolina."

It was announced on March 23 that General Conference would now be held in 2021, but specific dates would follow later. Bishop Leeland announced on the twenty-fourth that the suspension of in-person worship would continue until further notice. Governor Cooper on the

15. Michener, *The World is My Home*, 486.
16. Michener, *The World is My Home*, 485.

twenty-seventh issued a statewide stay-at-home order which prohibited gatherings of more than ten people and directed people to social distance.

On the third of April, the CDC recommended that Americans wear face coverings in public places, and that people should make their own masks at home and not buy surgical masks online or in the stores as there was a shortage. Those supplies were needed to be kept for the doctors, nurses, and other medical personnel that were caring for the public. The CDC also disclosed that the virus spreads aerially through conversation, singing, coughing, and by proximity. The news report that day stated that more than a quarter of a million Americans had been infected with this new virus and between six to seven thousand Americans have died.

As a pastoral and staff team, on all the Tuesdays that followed that first shut-down Tuesday, we moved as many of our ministries virtually as we could so that we would continue to disciple our communities. Youth Ministry started meeting by Zoom, as did Confirmation, other small group ministries, and church committees. Most of our Sunday School classes moved to Zoom as well. Other ministries were being done virtually: Bible Studies and Children's Ministries. In addition, we utilized Facebook for Thursday's Devotion and other teaching ministries. The pastors kept in contact with the congregation by making countless phone calls.

As a church, we wanted to feed people spiritually and physically. It was crucial to get our ministries virtual not only for our congregation but also for the people who in the midst of the pandemic would be looking for a word of hope. This storm shook people, letting loose waves upon waves of anxiety, fear, and isolation. We strived to provide a sense of hope and community for people who had suddenly lost their social anchors.

Some people who live alone go to the malls to be around other people. Some people go to restaurants and bars just to hear laughter and conversation. In almost a moment's time, all of those places were closed down. We, as a faith community, needed to keep in front of us the question: how do we build a bridge to all these people, to use Billy Joel's line, who are no longer able to share the drink called loneliness?[17]

As a team, we were aware that we live in an area that before the pandemic was marked by great food insecurity. The pandemic made this even worse. From the beginning of the storm, it was imperative for us to reach out and help meet those needs. We partnered with Second Harvest Food Bank, giving out countless meals. We also partnered with First Christian

17. Joel, *The Piano Man.*

and Children of Zion Ministries, extending our feeding ministry. In addition, our Sunday Schools collected tons of food for Crisis Control Ministry. There were many more ministry groups in the church than these distributing clothing and other forms of assistance. We also continued our strong financial support to area assistance ministries knowing that while their needs would be growing exponentially during this crisis, their donations would decline.

I mention all of these not to toot Main Street's horn, for all of the churches in Kernersville engaged in similar ministries. I mention it because in our society it is trendy to be critical of churches, especially among the cultural and political elites. What I want to say in response to that is, "Yes, people are made of clay." It does not matter where you find them. Whether in a political party, in Hollywood, in the media, in a university, in public schools, or in churches, people sin and sometimes sin greatly. Churches do not have the market cornered on the depravity of humanity, that is spread out evenly wherever one finds men and women. Still, despite the fallen nature of humanity, look at all the good that churches, synagogues, and mosques do in America. The good work they do by giving out bread to the hungry, by sharing words of encouragement and hope to those who are spiritually malnourished and providing a way for people to connect with each other and support one another.

On April 21, the announcement was made that General Conference would be held in Minneapolis from August 31 to September 10, 2021. The news was sure to be greeted by some with disappointment. What I also noticed among my parishioners, once the pandemic hit, was that General Conference was no longer on their minds. Everyone was too busy trying to make sense of and cope with the crisis in which we found ourselves.

On April 30, the news reported that the national shut-down guidelines from the White House were expiring, and there was a divide across the country on whether governors should extend the stay-at-home orders or not. Armed demonstrators descended on Michigan's Capitol grounds in Lansing to protest. Some of the armed protestors also paraded through the building and tried to force their way into the House Chamber. In one month, the death rate grew by a multiple of ten; now more than 62,000 Americans have died from the virus that we knew so little about on March 1. The news also reported on the toll that the pandemic exacted on doctors, nurses, and medical staff with a dramatic rise in depression, anxiety, distress, and insomnia among health care workers.

Chapter 9

ALDERSGATE, PENTECOST, AND THE DAYS OF SUMMER

MAY DAY, A FESTIVAL OF SPRING, can trace its roots back to the ancient Romans. As I drove around Kernersville on that Friday, I saw no celebrations of spring. The approaching days of summer were promising not relaxation and rest but anxiety, fear, and a rising cantankerousness across the country. Whatever spirit of unity that pulled the country together at first whereby people, generally, were tolerant of sheltering-in-place was dissipating.

As the storm continued to rage, what I already knew was deeply impressed upon me; we are a divided nation. Fox News told the pandemic story from their perspective, and CNN and other major news outlets told a different story. Tragically, amidst the greatest crisis that our country has faced since the Second World War, we, as a nation, could not find a way to turn our ideological swords into plowshares, working for the common good.

In those days, I heard a few individuals share that they thought the virus was a hoax, cooked up by Liberal Democrats who were attempting to crash the economy to ensure that Donald Trump would not be reelected as President. I had difficulty in those conversations. I wanted to ask, "Really, you believe that nonsense?" My daughter Laura, working as a Nurse at Baptist Hospital in Winston Salem, told me how awful it was to watch COVID-19 patients struggle to breathe. She and all the other health workers were risking their lives taking care of people valiantly fighting this disease and media personalities are misleading people into believing that this virus is a "Democratic Hoax" whose sole purpose is to deprive their President of a second term. Ministry has been affected by the non-regulated media platforms that can propagate any conspiracy theory making it sound as credible as Walter Cronkite.

Two months past the Ides of March and more than 85,000 Americans are dead. The Vietnam War (1964–1975) cost the lives of approximately 60,000 Americans. This war against COVID-19 in two months has exceeded the death rate of the Vietnam Conflict that lasted eleven years. Yet, there were a significant number of Americans refusing to believe that we were at war and that people were dying. How many times did I hear someone say that 50,000 die each year from the flu and that the death rate for the first half of 2019 and 2020 was comparable? People died so rapidly in New York from COVID-19 that the infrastructure could not keep pace. There were not enough portable morgues to park outside the hospitals, and mass burials on Hart Island was the answer to the question of what to do with all these dead bodies.

Amidst the pandemic, there were all the other regular happenings of the church calendar that needed to be observed in this most abnormal of times. Especially, I was mindful of the confirmands whose confirmation would now have to be postponed and of the graduating high school seniors who had already lost so many of the experiences that previous generations valued: sporting events, proms and, surprisingly enough, in-person classes. I heard from several youth that online school made it more difficult to accomplish the required work, for there seemed to be an amalgamation of home and school, a blurring of institutions that led for some not to greater efficiency but fatigue and despair.

The graduating seniors were on my mind when I composed the column for the church newsletter:

> Some of our most beloved children's literature utilize portals that transport the characters to another world. Alice falls down a rabbit hole into a subterranean place known as Wonderland. A cyclone sweeps Dorothy away from Kansas and takes her to the magical land of Oz. Peter, Susan, Edmund, and Lucy hide in an ordinary looking wardrobe that somehow magically enables them to stumble into a land called Narnia. In this genre of literature, there is a sudden disruption of ordinary life, and the protagonists undertake a journey that transforms them.

When the last semester of your academic year began, you had no idea the twists and the turns you would navigate and travel. You have gone from a pre-coronavirus realm to a land of social distancing; you have vacated the school building and conducted your education online; you have foregone rituals that you eagerly anticipated and adjusted to the demands of this new age. What you have learned in this journey strengthens you for what lies beyond.

Scripture assures us that no matter how strong the storm, God is with us in this world and the world to come. Jeremiah 29:11 states, "'For I know the plans I have for you,' declares the LORD, 'plans to prosper you and not to harm you, plans to give you hope and a future.'" Class of 2020, we are so incredibly proud of you, and we trust that God will direct and guide you on the journey you are called to travel.

On Memorial Day, I was thinking of previous generations that had also suffered through great disruptions in their lives. My father and uncles served in the Second World War while the families left behind waited with anxiety and fear, praying that their loved ones would one day return from the war. Reflecting on conversations with parishioners whose lives were greatly affected by sudden events beyond their control, I remembered Ruth.

Shortly after arriving at my first appointment, Cavanaugh United Methodist Church in Fort Smith, people warned me about Ruth. Some found her obnoxious; others had a fond endearment born out of sympathy. But they all agreed, "Preacher, she will kidnap you and not let you leave. It does not matter if you're visiting at her house or on the phone, she will hold you hostage. Be warned!" Truth be told, they were right. One person told me, "When Ruth calls, after listening for about twenty minutes, I carry the phone over to the front door quietly opening it and ring the doorbell saying, 'Oh Ruth, I am so sorry. Someone is here. I have got to go.'"

Ruth and I hit it off from the first. One of the reasons why is I have never been easily detained. When I needed to go, I would just say, "Got to go." Sometimes, she would still be talking as I left the house. But it was ok. We understood and appreciated one another. She knew I was not forged in the personality pleasing world of Methodist churches. As Garrison Keillor said, "We make fun of Methodists for their . . . fear of giving offense."[1]

Ruth did not have good social skills. She refused to take a hint. She would call people at 6 a.m. thinking they were just waiting for her call. I remember the one and only time she called me at that hour. Climbing out

---

1. Keillor, "Those People Called Methodists."

of the bed to answer the phone, nowhere close to having my first cup of coffee, I heard a cheerful voice say, "Yesterday, I was watching the news, and the commentator said . . . ." I interrupted, "Ruth, is this an emergency?" "No, pastor." "Ruth, don't call me at 6 a.m. unless it's an emergency." She said, "Okay, pastor." She was good as her word and never called before 8 a.m. from that day forward. I thought 8 a.m. was way too early, but I did not have the heart to say 9 a.m.

Ruth did not have many friends apart from the church, and her only child lived eight-hundred miles away. I loved Ruth, but she was cantankerous. This scene was replayed again and again. Standing on her front porch, seeing her through the screen door, sitting at the kitchen table, with an oxygen tank, wearing a nasal cannula, and underneath it a lit cigarette, I would call out, "Ruth, you're not smoking in there, are you?" And she would yell back, "Lordy no preacher." She did not realize I could see her putting the cigarette out and waving her hand around trying to dissipate the smoke.

Ruth told me about her life, about her late husband who was a prisoner in a Japanese concentration camp on an island in the Pacific. He referred to it as a god-forsaken place, and a few other words that I will not chronicle. Ruth went into detail about the cruelty of the Japanese soldiers. There he was beaten and starved. There he almost died. She told me that when the war was over and he was free again, he devoured the first steak he got in almost one bite. Though freed from that camp, the nightmares lived with him for years, haunting his soul while he slept. She cared for him and lived through his terrors. I wondered, what emotional price had she paid loving him as fiercely as she did?

Frequently she said to me with a chuckle, "Michael, die young, while you're still beautiful, so the world will mourn your passing." Ruth not only gave me unsolicited advice but also revealed, in her opinion, that the world did not care or celebrate people like her. When I conducted her funeral, I could not help but feel that people like Ruth deserve their own day; a day to honor those who have suffered long and hard with their loved ones who returned from war, wounded in more ways than we can ever imagine. We decorate our soldiers with ribbons and medals, throw them parades, have them stand up in church on the eleventh hour of the eleventh day of the eleventh month, but fail to adequately support them with their life sentence of struggling with the memories of the hell that they endured.

When the Japanese bombed Pearl Harbor on December 7, 1941, President Franklin Roosevelt did not have any major obstacles standing in the way of declaring war on the Japanese. The newspapers and news reels were full of images of the bombing of Pearl Harbor, images of burning ships and bodies. It was far easier to mobilize the American public to combat an enemy that could be seen than to wage war against an unseen combatant. A war against an unseen enemy living in your own house or neighborhood is a tough sell to a people who have been indoctrinated by a consumeristic society that they can have it their way.

The virus was not the only disruption on Memorial Day. The same day I am remembering Ruth from the long ago past, the television brought horrific images to my mind that were happening on a Minneapolis street so many miles away. George Floyd, a North Carolina native, an African American, was senselessly killed by Derek Chauvin, a police officer who was sworn to protect. He cut short the life of a forty-six-year-old man who had plenty of life in front of him. On a street surrounded by other police officers and a crowd of spectators, Floyd cried out, "I can't breathe." For approximately nine minutes, Chauvin kept his knee on Floyd's throat. Chauvin's inhumanity seared the American conscience.

What a span of eight days! On the United Methodist calendar, May 24 is marked as Aldersgate Day when John Wesley, the founder of Methodism, had an experience of God that so revolutionized his life that it propelled him to expand his evangelistic ministry. On Memorial Day (May 25), while remembering the nation's dead who gave their lives in service to their country, we were shocked by a video of a police officer extinguishing the life of a fellow citizen for no warranted reason. On the thirty-first of May, the church calendar was Pentecost Sunday, and the liturgical color of the day was red. Between Aldersgate Day and Pentecost Sunday, the nation struggled with what was versus what should have been.

On Pentecost Sunday, I was mindful of the confirmands who could not be with us in worship. We would later have an in-person outdoor Confirmation service in the Paul J. Ciener Botanical Garden in August where we would lay hands on them praying the epiclesis, asking the Spirit of God to descend upon them.

Confirmation Sunday, whether in a pandemic or not, always recalls the memory of my Confirmation in the Abbey Church of Subiaco. I still remember the weight of Bishop Andrew McDonald's hands as he prayed the epiclesis. I still remember the solemnity that hung in the air, and the majesty of it all with the bishop looking so regal. Of course, it is not like I had met many bishops in my childhood. The only other one was Fulton Sheen.

I preached on that pandemic Pentecost from Acts 2:1-21. Pentecost is the birthday of the church. On that day, so long ago, the Holy Spirit descended on the Apostles and disciples with divided tongues of fire, and they began to speak in foreign languages. Devout Jews from all over the world gathered in Jerusalem for the Jewish Festival of Pentecost (Shavuot), a pilgrim feast that celebrated the first fruits of the harvest. They asked,

> "Are not all these who are speaking Galileans? And how is it that we hear, each of us, in our own native language? Parthians, Medes, Elamites, and residents of Mesopotamia, Judea and Cappadocia, Pontus and Asia, Phrygia and Pamphylia, Egypt and the parts of Libya belonging to Cyrene, and visitors from Rome, both Jews and proselytes Cretans and Arabs—in our own languages we hear them speaking about God's deeds of power." All were amazed and perplexed, saying to one another, "What does this mean?"[2]

After debunking the accusation of drunkenness, Peter started to preach and preach he did. On the birthday of the church, God poured out the Holy Spirit on the people of all nations. The Gospel of Christ is for all, and yet America still struggles with its original sin.[3]

Amidst the national tragedy, President Trump seemed incapable of leading the nation in collective grief. This was not new. He also failed to be a healing presence when racial strife erupted in Charlottesville in August of 2017. When the riots broke out across the country after George Floyd's death, Trump exacerbated the troubles by resharing an old slogan that was utilized by racist politicians in the 1960s; "When the looting starts, the shooting starts." When the riots happened in DC, the military was mobilized with low flying helicopters meant to intimidate the crowds, a fence was built around the White House, and military troops in battle gear lined up in front of the Lincoln Memorial. Lincoln, the great unifier, and healer must have been rolling in his grave. James Mattis, a retired four-star Marine General who had also served previously in the Trump administration as Secretary of Defense wrote, "Donald Trump is the first president in my lifetime who does not try to unite the American people—does not even pretend to try. Instead, he tries to divide us."[4]

---

2. Acts 2:7b–12 (NRSV).

3. See Wallis, *America's Original Sin*.

4. Goldberg, "James Mattis Denounces President Trump, Describes Him as a Threat to the Constitution."

On the front cover of the June issue of *Der Spiegel* magazine were these words: "*Der Feuerteufel: Ein Präsident setzt sein Land in Brand,*" which translates as: "The Fire Devil: A President Sets Fire to his Country." The cover featured Donald Trump sitting in the Presidential Office holding a match while out of the windows of the White House, raging fires burned, and riot police and the protesting crowds navigated the smoke and flames. The article captured well the American predicament:

> The U.S. has been beset by a perfect storm. In absolute numbers, no other industrialized country has been hit as hard by the coronavirus pandemic as the United States, with more than 100,000 dead. The economic consequences of the virus have also been devastating: More than 40 million Americans have lost their jobs, a disaster second only to the Great Depression. And now, the killing of George Floyd has torn open the country's oldest wound: the deep-seated racism left behind by slavery.[5]

Fires burning across the country, mass protests from shore to shore and, as Mattis communicated, the President is deliberately dividing the nation.

On June 1, in the Main Street Community Garden, Wayne Purdy, the Director of Youth Ministries witnessed an act of racism by a stranger who had come to the Garden seeking assistance. Wayne and his team were handing out assistance to those in need. The seeker of assistance refused to accept a food bag from an African American who was helping to distribute needed goods. The European American middle-aged woman uttered some reprehensible verbiage. When Wayne told me what had transpired, he and I were shocked and incredulous that in the twenty-first century in the pleasant community of Kernersville such a racist incident could still occur. When I shared this story with a few African Americans friends who live in Kernersville, they registered no surprise whatsoever. It is such a temptation for someone like me who has read about the history, art, music, and cultural changes of the 1960s to deceive myself into thinking that the battle for racial justice was won by Martin Luther King Jr., Lyndon Johnson, Bobby Kennedy, and millions of others who marched and fought for equality, rather than the reality that the war is never completely over. Hatred can take up residence in the human heart no matter what age it is.

Also in June, the Kernersville Christian Ministers' Fellowship started discussing over the next several months *Woke Church* by Eric Mason. The Fellowship sought to understand the great divide that exists when it comes

---

5. Mingels et al., "A Perfect Storm."

to conversations about race relations and racial reconciliation and what we can do as pastors and churches to build a bridge to a more just future.

On Sunday evening (June 28), NBC News reported that Alex Azar (Health and Human Services Secretary) issued a disconcerting and rather frightening warning that the window for the nation to contain the virus was closing. Thirteen states reversed their opening up plans due to a resurgence of the virus. The Texas outbreak increased so dramatically that the hospital system was quickly becoming overwhelmed. There was also a feature on Coach Mike Krzyzewski of Duke University powerfully denouncing racism. He invited the viewer to say it with him: "Black Lives Matter." President Trump, on the other hand, retweeted a racist video that the White House took down after complaints were made. Voices in the crowd (of the video that the President retweeted) chanted, "White Power." By June 30, approximately 130,000 Americans had died from COVID-19.

In July, we had a staff member test positive. Thankfully, he had a mild case. The church leadership closed the office down for two weeks and instructed the staff to work remotely.

Thom Rainer on his blog posted an article July 26 on "Ten Reasons Why Your Church Members Are Ornery in the Pandemic." The post listed reasons why you would expect parishioners in a pandemic to be cantankerous: weary, confused, fearful, feel like they are losing their church, cultural fights, stressed over the politics of a presidential season, negativity on social media, miss their friends, loss of outward focus, and routines disrupted.[6] I was not surprised by the increase of complaints that occurred as the storm continued. The spirit of unity that pulled the congregation together at the beginning of the storm waned.

I resonated with Rainer's article not just due to church life, but also because of all the lamentations storming across the landscape of my own mind like buffaloes across the plains. Sometimes after a long day at the church, I would collapse in my comfortable chair in my home office. As I let the laments roam around in my mind, I felt guilty about indulging in my complaints. Amidst a global pandemic with the economies of the world in freefall and with countless numbers of people across our country and world in ICU units fighting for their lives, I remained gainfully employed and healthy enough. It was nervy of me to register my objections with God, yet I would be inauthentic if I did not admit that I too was full of protestation.

---

6. Rainer, "Ten Reasons Why Your Church Members Are Ornery in the Pandemic."

I fussed because the Bruce Cockburn concert scheduled for May 14 in Raleigh in which I had front row seats was cancelled. I had planned like a groupie to present my album of *Dancing in the Dragon's Jaws* for his signature and gush on and on about how I sang his songs when I once lived in Canada. Rhonda takes issue with that statement. She corrects me saying, "You didn't live there. You were just visiting." I believe sojourning in the great white north for over two months qualifies me for almost denizen status. I had even been communicating with Cockburn's manager on Messenger about whether it would be possible to have Bruce sign the album. The manager assured me there would be no problem.

I also lodged my grievance about how our planned trip to Saratoga Springs, New York, to see my long-time friend from university days (Andrew) had to be postponed to a futuristic day too futuristic to see. Furthermore, he had gotten great tickets for us to see Bob Dylan in Saratoga on the ninth of July. I had no illusions about the possibility of getting Dylan's signature on an album. Having attended previous Dylan concerts, he magically appears on stage and just as mysteriously disappears, rarely even communicating, other than in song, with the audience. The Dylan concert was cancelled along with all the other trips and concerts that I had planned to do in 2020. Also, I had running around in my mind about a fall trip to cash in my airline miles. Where would I go this time? Maybe to Wales to climb Garth Mountain. Melancholic, frustrated, I spent a lot of time watching *Rick Steves' Europe* reruns.

In conversations with pastor friends, they lamented the loss of supportive in-person fellowship with other ministers. District Meetings had already been greatly diminished when the Western North Carolina Conference some years before the pandemic for financial reasons, redrew the map and went from fifteen districts down to eight. And of course, amidst the pandemic, Annual Conference scheduled for June was postponed to August. What would normally be almost a weeklong meeting of clergy and laity, reconnecting with friends from previous churches and colleagues from previous districts, and catching up with friends from years gone by, was transformed into a few hours of a Zoom meeting listening to the talking heads. Suddenly preachers were asking, "Now, whom do I share the drink called loneliness with?"

Sometimes in the orbit of the Robert Schullers and Norman Vincent Peales of this world, complaints get painted negatively. The prosperity gospel preachers take it even a step further by arguing that the complainer is bringing their reality forth with their words, and if they just had enough faith their conditions would change. Contrary to those opinions, the Scriptures instruct us that it is important to register our griefs and our losses. The Psalmist models for us how important it is to direct our anger at God and not to withhold from our Heavenly Father our rage. The Psalmist cried out, "My God, my God, why have you forsaken me?"[7] As evidenced by the Book of Lamentations, it is deeply ingrained in the biblical tradition that we take to God all of our sorrows, disruptions, national and global upheavals, and personal crises. The writer of Lamentations chisels into the stones of time the bitterness over the fall of Jerusalem (God's holy city) in 587 BC.

Responding to the requests from parishioners for opportunities to fellowship, we planned three Sunday evening services in August in the Paul J. Ciener Botanical Garden inviting people to bring a lawn chair, wear their masks, socially distance, and enjoy fellowship with one another. One evening service was a Back-to-School service lifting words of hope and prayer for the beginning of another school year plagued by the coronavirus. One Sunday evening service, we confirmed the Confirmands. And one service was dedicated to singing old-time Gospel hymns along with preaching. We continued Sunday morning services as live stream only.

The news for August 31 reported that there have now been more than six million coronavirus cases in the U.S., and 183,000 have died from the virus. Kenosha, Wisconsin, was in turmoil from a police shooting of an African American. On August 23, Jacob Blake, while resisting arrest, was shot multiple times. This was followed by riots, violence, and more death. President Trump announced his intention to visit the state. Governor Tony Evers asked Trump not to visit Kenosha fearing that the President would inflame the situation even more leading to greater racial strife. Riots were occurring in Portland, Oregon, and in other cities across the nation. The news also reported that violent crime rates had risen by more than 50 percent from last year.

7. Psalm 22:1a (NRSV).

Chapter 10

Dueling Politicians
and a Rising Death Count

As September 2020 began, what I never thought possible in March was now so very true: the six-month pandemic was nowhere close to winding down. Back in March, the pandemic seemed so far away from Kernersville. It was a viral outbreak that was occurring in New York and New Jersey. But as the months passed, it became very near to us as well. Parishioners contracted the coronavirus, and the majority got better after a couple of weeks, but not everyone. Death was made even more difficult by COVID-19. People died in ICU units that were closed to pastors, family, and friends visiting. As the seriously ill waged a losing battle against the virus, loved ones from their homes had to share lasting parting words over a phone to one that they would never see in this life again. Funerals were conducted outdoors or in funeral homes. We still had not opened the sanctuary for in-person services of any kind. Like the preceding months, September was defined by the pandemic, racial strife, and by gladiatorial political combat.

On September 1, Keith Vereen and I did what countless clergy across the nation did in that moment. We tried to build bridges. We began a six-week course on Eric Mason's book *Woke Church*. Keith is the pastor of Providence Baptist Church, an African American congregation. We limited the class to ten from each church (Main Street UMC and Providence Baptist) so that we could have time for everyone to contribute to the conversation.

I was amazed that in our very first meeting people forthrightly shared the pain that they had experienced from being judged not by "the content of their character" but by "the color of their skin." Individuals told heartbreaking stories of being stopped by the police for no reason. And I pondered how I have traveled far and wide for decades and have only been detained once in my life and that was by Czechoslovakian Border Guards who took issue with the evangelistic efforts in which my friends and I were engaged.

On September 8, President Donald Trump made a campaign stop in Winston-Salem and one of my parishioners made the news. Before the Campaign Rally, Dave Plyler, the Republican Chairman of the Forsyth County Board of Commissioners, was asked if he thought Trump should abide by Governor Roy Cooper's order that people should wear a mask in public gatherings. Plyler responded, "It's been ordered by the governor. When in Rome, do as the Romans do. When in North Carolina, do as the governor says."[1] Plyler continued, "He (Trump) is a citizen of the United States, but he is also a guest in our county. Without a mask, he could get sick, and he could blame the governor."[2] Tickets were required to attend the event but, ironically, before one could register for it, one had to release the Trump campaign and the airport from any liability for exposure to COVID.[3]

A little less than a week later, the long-awaited parking lot was finally completed. Due to construction, it had been torn up since May. We had our first outdoor worship service on September 13. Additional outdoor services followed on the twentieth and the twenty-seventh. It was great to be able to worship in-person again, and we were blessed that the rain did not fall on any of those three Sundays. People were hungry to see each other. Of course, prior to the first service we instructed the congregation to wear masks and to socially distance.

Ruth Bader Ginsburg, the legendary Supreme Court Justice, died on September 18 at the age of 87. On September 26, President Trump held an outdoor ceremony and news conference to formally announce his nomination (Amy Coney Barrett) for the vacant Supreme Court position. At that time, large gatherings were banned in Washington, DC, but since the

1. Hinton, "President Trump should wear a mask during his visit to Winston-Salem, county Republican says."

2. Hinton, "President Trump should wear a mask during his visit to Winston-Salem, county Republican says."

3. Hinton, "President Trump should wear a mask during his visit to Winston-Salem, county Republican says."

White House is federal property, the event was exempted from local mandates. More than a hundred and fifty attendees were present, and the great majority did not wear masks or socially-distance. There was no shortage of congratulatory handshakes and hugs that day. A significant number of individuals who attended the event later tested positive for COVID-19. Dr. Anthony Fauci referred to it as a "superspreader event."

The political polarization took its toll on relationships between family members, friends, and parishioners. Common-sense and compassionate actions, like wearing a mask to protect others from any possible exposure that one might have had to the sometimes-deadly coronavirus, became viewed through the lens of American politics. If one wore a mask, someone would contend that you had drunk the Democratic Kool-Aid. If you refused to wear a mask, then others deduced that you must be a devotee of President Trump.

The political cult of personality is certainly not new, but it is a distraction from the issues that have enormous consequences for our lives and for the health of the planet. What matters for the Christian would be to vote for the candidate who most closely aligns with Jesus's values. Each person must weigh those sacred loyalties when entering the sanctuary of the voting booth.

The Church Council met on September 24 and voted to open the sanctuary on October 4 for in-person worship. The lay leadership wanted to ensure that we were doing all that we could to protect our parishioners and visitors from COVID-19. To ensure that we did not have a superspreader event, the church employed stringent health and safety measures.

On the last day of September, the news reported that the Presidential Debate from the night before was so full of interruptions, name-calling, and truculent behavior that the Commission on Presidential Debates said that they would make changes before the next debate. One possible solution under consideration is to turn off the microphone of a candidate when it is not his turn to speak. Trump claimed on the thirtieth that he had won the debate, even though the national polls suggested the opposite. A particularly painful moment occurred during the debate when Trump struggled to denounce "White Nationalism." When pushed by Fox News anchor Chris Wallace to condemn the "Proud Boys," Trump said, "Proud Boys, stand back and stand by." The Proud Boys did not receive it as a condemnation, and the next day they were using the President's words as a marketing tool, a rallying cry, and a new logo. It was reminiscent of the

President's response to Charlottesville when he said, "Very fine people on both sides." If the President of the United States is not committed to work for unity, reconciliation, peace, and goodwill, then the country will begin to resemble what the President is elevating: strife, animosity, villainizing opponents, and winner take all.

The news reported that Trump was also sowing seeds of doubt about the legitimacy of the upcoming election. He said, "This is going to be a fraud like you have never seen." Trump claimed that the source of the fraud would be with the mail-in-ballots. Other stories of the day were as follows: airline travel is down 70 percent, and the airlines argued that if Congress did not give them another bailout, they would be forced to lay off around 50,000 workers. It was also announced that Disney had laid off 28,000 individuals. Wildfires in Northern California were destroying wineries and vineyards in Napa Valley. More than 206,000 Americans had died from COVID-19, and more than 7 million had contracted the virus.

By the fourth of October, it seemed as if we were learning how to navigate the pandemic. Life can now move somewhat back to normal. Well, perhaps as normal as it can be after a devastating and world-wide plague. Will we ever get anywhere close to life before the pandemic, or will that remain an elusive dream? I had no answer, but at least we were now able to gather again in the sanctuary. As already mentioned, we did not have congregational singing. And yes, no common cup or loaves were used for World Communion Sunday. We had to acclimatize ourselves to those not so easy to open, self-contained, Eucharistic packages that probably have enough preservatives in them to last until Christ's Second Coming. Yet, it was glorious to see all the faces there hidden behind the masks.

With the election approximately two weeks away, I thought back to another day, so many years ago. It was the 1980s. Sitting in Re-Pete's, a hamburger joint in Fort Smith, I was having lunch with Joe, a parishioner. He, a highly successful businessman, multi-millionaire, and a colorful character, was known in the corridors of power in my home state. All kinds of legends surrounded him including escaping from a Central American or South American jail. My memory fails to remember which it was.

After Bill Clinton lost the governorship in 1981, he spent the next two years traveling the state preparing for another run. Joe and his wife Ramona spent some time going along on those ventures as encouraging friends. When Joe and I got the idea in 1990 to invite Sheffield Nelson and Bill Clinton to have a political debate hosted at Cavanaugh United Methodist

Church, it was Joe that the handlers called to decline our thoughtful request. I did not even get a rejection letter. Had I gotten one, I would have framed it and hung it on a prominent wall.

After we had given our order to the waitress, Joe said, "Pastor, I just don't know anymore. I was raised to respect Congressmen and Senators. They were my heroes. They were the people who went into government to serve the people. And the President, I was taught as a kid, was the best of all, the most noble, and the smartest." Taking a sip of his Diet Coke, he then said, "But I just don't know. I don't like watching those biography shows anymore."

Fresh out of seminary with my newly minted Master of Divinity, I had more knowledge than common sense. I launched into an expansive discourse on why I love those biography shows. "Did you see the one about Franklin Delano Roosevelt and his mistress? What about Eisenhower and the female chauffeur? That is one way to stave off the cold English nights. Or did you see the one on Johnson? Oh, my Lord, that man. And need we even talk about JFK? Of course, then there was Nixon and Watergate, and Reagan and Iran Contra."

As I traveled down that road, he looked, more and more, like a man living in a land devoid of heroes. It dawned on me that we were, most assuredly, from two different generations. He was born during the Great Depression, and I was born somewhere at the end of the Baby Boomers and the beginning of Gen X. We saw the world differently. His generation made heroes of political and military leaders, and my generation made heroes of rock stars and athletes. His generation expected the heroes to live morally exemplary lives, and my generation's heroes suffered from overdoses, serial relationships, and materialistic excess. We did not expect our heroes to be virtuous. We expected them to connect with us, to inspire us, and to perform feats of greatness. Truly, the landscape of America changed in just a few decades.

Corporate America and its marketing agents are busy at work fashioning idols of one sort or another. The music industry, the NBA, the NFL, the MLB, Hollywood, Madison Avenue, and political machines are busy creating larger than life personalities. They craft compelling narratives for the person of the moment that we should, if not bow down to, attend their concerts, and lay our money down for their albums, or attend their games and buy their jerseys and sneakers. And for the politicians, not only do they want us to give them our vote and make large cash donations, but to also purchase bumper stickers, yards signs, masks, and t-shirts with their names blazoned upon them. Attempting to seduce us into believing that they alone, like a mythic hero of old, can fix the problems that ail us. John Calvin, the sixteenth century Swiss Reformer, said, "The human heart is an idol making factory." Moses learned that when he stayed up on Mount Sinai just a little too long.

I am now about the age that Joe was when we had lunch together so long ago in RePete's. If I were meeting with a young freshly minted graduate of a seminary, and she or he asked me my opinion of the politicians of the moment, would I have any wisdom to offer or would I utter a long elegy on the loss of heroes?

There were now three days left to one of the most contested, troubled, bellicose American presidential elections. Joe Biden's and Donald Trump's campaigns were pulling out all the stops. Contending that the doctors are inflating the number of COVID cases, Trump said, "You know our doctors get more money if somebody dies from COVID." Again, I thought of my daughter and all other medical care workers standing in the gap between us and this terrible virus. I could not understand how the President of the United States could make such an outrageous claim. This is not politics; this is a war against a deadly virus. More than 230,000 Americans had already died from COVID-19. We were now closing in on losing four times the number of Americans killed in the Vietnam War. In other news of the day, England locked down again over rising COVID rates. There were also fears that Halloween would be another superspreader event.

Finally, the long-anticipated day arrived, November 3. Those Americans who had not mailed in their ballots were asked to stand in long lines until they finally could enter a voting booth and vote; vote for the candidate which they thought would be the best choice for the president and vote as well for all the other offices that were on the ballot. Voters were not asked if they thought that Donald Trump and Joseph Biden represented the very best possible choice out of 331 million citizens to be the leader of the free world. My ideal presidential choice would be President Jed Bartlet, a Nobel Prize winning economist, former university professor, who was drawn into the political fray out of a desire to work for the common good. Bartlet, a professing Christian, allowed his Roman Catholic faith to inform his political judgments. Unfortunately, Bartlet was a character played by the actor Martin Sheen on a Burbank set. All of us who measure our political candidates against the canon of Jed Bartlet are bound to be disappointed.

Many clergy are criticized by their parishioners for building a wall between the church and the political world. They critique their pastor for not speaking prophetically to the issues of the day. Other laity, in the very same church, caution their pastor not to speak to the issues of the day for fear of upsetting other parishioners and the risk of jeopardizing worship attendance and budget capacity. The pastor is caught in the middle feeling at times like a ping pong ball.

It is true that clergy are already facing a tsunami of cultural wars and ecclesiastical changes. One should not by any means be surprised when a pastor tries to find a solution that makes all sides of the political spectrum satisfied. Yet, Jesus did not equivocate. He said, "You shall love the Lord your God with all your heart, and with all your soul, and with all your mind."[4] That means that Christians are not in the idol construction business, whether it be the idols of institutional Christianity or the idols of American civil religion. We should lift high the cross for all to see. We should resolutely proclaim that the standard is Christ our Lord.

Through the years, I have voted for Republican and Democratic candidates, and I expected the same of my parishioners. Vote for the person who is closest to the values of Jesus, I would counsel parishioners when asked. Vote for the candidate who cares about the least and the broken. Vote for the candidate who believes government should help the homeless, the mentally and emotionally troubled, the addicts, and the many veterans suffering from PTSD. Vote for the candidate who cares about what Jesus cared about: the orphans, the widows, the poor, the immigrants, the dispossessed, and the ones that society cast aside and rejected. I realize that almost sounds like the butt of a joke: core values, politicians, and Jesus walked into a bar. But one sorts through the candidates and does the best one can when entering the voting booth.

On November 4, the outcome of the presidential race was still undecided. Joe Biden led in the electoral college vote with 253 votes to Trump's 214. Trump had falsely declared himself the winner. All the while, he continued to pontificate that there was widespread voter fraud even though no evidence was forthcoming. Interestingly enough, Trump did not contend that there was fraud in all of the elections in which the Republicans won Senate and House seats. Pennsylvania, North Carolina, and Georgia were all still too early to call. Trump's campaign continued to file and threaten to file lawsuits contesting the legitimacy of the election in specific states. The

---

4. Matthew 22:37 (NRSV).

good news of the election is the country enjoyed the highest voter turnout in more than a century.

The counts and the recounts would continue as the days turned into weeks, all the while the country continued to suffer under the scourge of the largest pandemic since the 1918 and 1919 worldwide influenza outbreak. In the November newsletter, I wrote about a good friend who had recently died from COVID-19:

> Her husband went to a luncheon. He caught the virus from someone at that meeting, and his symptoms were mild. Sadly, she caught it from her husband, had severe symptoms, struggled mightily in the ICU, fighting it, but could not overcome. I mention this to remind everyone to stay vigilant. We have all heard the nonsense that the pandemic would go away just as soon as the election was over—that the pandemic is manufactured by the media—and even though, all this conspiracy absurdity is out there on different media platforms, my friend is still dead. Not from old age, not from other medical conditions, she was in relatively good health. She died from COVID-19.
>
> We, Christians, are called to speak the truth, and we are called to practice the Golden Rule. We cannot let our guards down. Experts are calling for a second wave as we approach winter. We must continue to social distance, wear the mask, have our temperatures taken, and be proactive for our neighbor's health and for our own. I understand that we are all fatigued by this pandemic, that we miss what life was like pre-pandemic. And though there is encouraging news on the vaccine front, it will be a while before it can be distributed to the entire country.

After concluding my article, I sat in my office staring out the window struggling to make sense of how what we used to regard as an innocent Men's Luncheon became the mechanism that led to my friend's death. I received an email on November 18 from the Forsyth County Department of Health notifying me that we had a COVID-19 outbreak in one of our Sunday School classes that was meeting outdoors in a local park. The members of the class who contracted the virus had relatively mild cases.

The Center of Disease Control recommended on the nineteenth that Americans should not travel for Thanksgiving. If you did choose to visit family, the CDC provided these guidelines: wear a mask, socially distance, bring your own food, drinks, plates, utensils, disposable containers, single-use salad dressings, condiments, and refrain from congregating in the kitchen as well as other recommendations. Despite the precautions, the infection rate continued. At the end of November, the nation faced a new COVID explosion. Concerned over the effects of Thanksgiving travel, of families and friends getting together to celebrate and to give thanks, gathering to feast on turkey and cranberries, Fauci predicted that the country will experience a surge upon a surge.

In the month of November, there were over four million new cases of COVID and more than 35,000 new fatalities. Hospitals in many cities were once again at capacity level. More than 267,000 Americans have died from the virus that we, the American public, knew so little about on March 1. There was good news on the vaccine front as Pfizer and Moderna vaccines were seeking approval from the government for widespread use. On the political front, Joe Biden received his first classified briefing, and President Trump continued to make unfounded claims of election fraud. The certified voting results from Arizona and Wisconsin sealed Biden's victory.

I looked through old photo albums and read my travel diaries from so long ago. I missed traveling. I missed the open road, watching telephone poles pass by in my peripheral vision. I missed the train rides from Manchester to Grindleford. I longed for bustling airports with a plane ready to take me (almost magically) to a new land. I was grateful that Rhonda and I in late October and early November of 2019 traveled following in the footsteps of the Apostle Paul. I remembered those nights on the balcony of our cabin, listening to the Aegean, talking about our dreams and hopes for the future. Looking through the old photo albums, I wondered just how long it would be until we felt safe to travel again.

Chapter 11

No Room at the Inn Revisited
Christmastide and Epiphany

THE CHURCH COUNCIL MET on December 3. After hearing a presentation on the rising COVID-19 rates in Forsyth County and after much robust discussion, the Council voted (by no means unanimous) to shut down in-person worship and revert to livestream worship only. The decision was made to ensure the safety of our parishioners and visitors and out of a concern for all of those standing in the gap fighting this terrible virus. The rising rates were not limited to our county. By December 2, there were around 14 million COVID-19 cases in the United States and more than 274,000 individuals had died from the virus. On that day alone, there were over 205,000 new cases. The hospitals and medical workers were struggling.

Returning to livestream only worship in Advent was a painful decision. Realizing that on Christmas Eve the doors of the sanctuary would be closed for in-person worship brought a new depth of meaning to the expression that there was "no room in the inn." Christmas Eve, one of the holiest nights of the year, and the sanctuary will not be the gathering spot for far flung families to come together, to sing Christmas hymns, to partake of the cup and bread, and to raise lit candles high for all to see. Instead, many will gather with their families and watch it together from the comfort of home. Others, having no one to share the service with will have to watch it alone on their TV, laptop, tablet, or iPhone while sitting on a chair.

Even though, as already mentioned, I do not like to think of myself as an institutionalist, the truth is institutional concerns are never far from my mind. As I sat there in the Church Council meeting knowing that the right decision to be made was to revert to livestream only, my mind wondered, "By how much will the pandemic accelerate the decline of an already declining denomination?" Furthermore, and closer to home, "What will the effect of this long raging storm be on Main Street UMC?" So many of my parishioners had been incredibly faithful and loyal to the church during the pandemic, but will this second shut-down lead to such frustrations that they will go to the churches in Kernersville and the surrounding area who have been having in-person worship for the last seven or eight months? I knew the answer already. I understood that when I voted "yes" to shut down again we would be losing families out the back door.

After the church council meeting on the third, there was palpable frustration. No one got in my face taunting me with, "Preacher, where is your faith?" I did not receive any disrespectful texts, emails, or phone calls. I need to take a moment to brag on my parishioners for even though many disagreed with the decision they never became disagreeable. Well, at least, that I knew of. Of course, it is possible that I was burned in effigy in remote and not so remote parts of Forsyth County. It is conceivable that there were photoshopped pictures of me looking like the Grinch hanging next to manger scenes or attached to dart boards. But if any of that occurred, word never got to me. My experience was not identical to that of all preachers. One of my friends in a church council meeting had someone point blank question his faith for attempting to protect his parishioners and visitors from this potentially deadly virus.

When my parishioners shared with me their frustration, I commiserated for I was just as frustrated as they were. I wanted nothing more than to go back to those glory days of shaking hands, hugging, patting people on the back, telling tall tales in the narthex, and receiving a kiss or two. By this point in the pandemic, we had all long since passed the great fatigue of having one's life interrupted and shut down by this plague. We were hungry for normalcy. For those who were fortunate enough not to catch the virus, and for those who did not end up in an ICU unit struggling for breath, the shutdown appeared to make no sense.

On December 6, like so many other preachers across the country, I preached on the lectionary text of Mark 1:1–8 detailing the activities of Jesus's cousin, John the Baptist. Here we were struggling with pandemic isolation, and there was John flourishing in the Judean wilderness. He lived a simple life as a prophet, teacher, and herald of a long-expected Messiah. Wearing a camel's hair garment with a leather belt around his waist, he subsisted on a diet of locusts and wild honey. He did not need to make an appearance on TV shows about decluttering and downsizing. Though he owned almost no possessions, his fame spread throughout the country. His name was known in the palace, in the cities, and in the countryside; even the first century historian Josephus mentioned him.

John's message was not just theological but also political; prepare the way for the Lord, the new Davidic king. Prepare the way for the one who will bring in the Messianic Age. Make his paths straight. The King is coming, and people need to make ready. If one ushers in a new kingdom, it goes without saying that the old one will be discarded. Herod Antipas, Tetrarch of Galilee and Perea, did not eagerly look forward to becoming yesterday's news.

John preached a message of repentance and baptized with water. The Greek word for repent means to change one's mind, to change one's directions, to turn around. Sometimes the kindest thing you can do is to tell someone that they are traveling in the wrong direction and that the only way that they can arrive at their desired destination is to turn around and go in opposite direction. But will we have ears to hear if someone tells us that we made a mistake? Or will we dismiss the messenger and the word of judgment?

The rich and the poor, the powerful and the oppressed, were told by John that they needed to prepare the way for the one who was yet to make his entrance upon the world's stage, the one more powerful than the messenger. John spent his days telling people get ready, to make room, to make space in their hearts and lives for the coming Lord. It is so much easier as a preacher to tell others to make room than it is to do so oneself.

Not everyone listening to John's words calling for repentance in the first century repented. And not everyone does today either. Not everyone who receives the notification that they are walking in the wrong direction turns around and travels in the right direction. When confronted with the truth that we have missed the mark, is it not amazing how many rationalizations flood through our minds? Frederick Herzog often said, "It's not about talking the talk. It's about walking the walk."[1] As a preacher, I have found myself talking a good game but struggling to live out the words I proclaimed. John's words cascade down through the centuries and convict me again and again.

In the sermon that day, I shared the story of one who struggled to understand what judgment meant in one's life. Long before he was elected to the American Academy of Arts and Sciences—prior to winning a Pulitzer Prize—before he won a MacArthur Fellowship—prior to receiving one of the nation's highest civilian honors (the Presidential Medal of Freedom)—before he won the National Humanities Medal—long before he wrote the popular and widely read children's book, *The Story of Ruby Bridges*—long before any of that, Robert Coles was not much more than a newly minted MD doing a psychiatric residence. He was most definitely wet behind the ears.

The patient was a 25-year-old graduate student in literature. She temporarily left Coles speechless, which is no easy feat for a man so gifted with words. The presenting problem was that she possessed guilty feelings that would not go away. Coles tried to talk to her about it being an irrational response. The woman had an improper relationship with her employer, and Coles kept trying to focus on the unconscious significance of the affair. But she would not let go of it, and one day she said to him, "You keep trying to find the cause of my difficulty within me; but I believe there's someone else who has to be mentioned."[2] He asked her if she had anyone particular in mind. She wanted to answer "God" but feared Coles might have questioned her sanity, so she answered indirectly.

Coles was at a loss. He needed clarification, and he communicated that to her. She stated firmly, "It is sin I'm talking about."[3] And Coles who had been steeped in the psychological reductionism of his discipline and age, sat puzzled, scratching his head. He then asked her what sin had to do with her depression that threatened to overwhelm her. Coles wrote:

> I remember thinking to myself that she was, perhaps, sicker than I'd first realized, that (at the least) she was using a religious term to avoid discussing some quite serious and painful psychological

---

1. Frederick Herzog (1925–1995) taught theology at Duke University from 1960 until his death in 1995.

2. Coles, *Harvard Diary*, 100.

3. Coles, *Harvard Diary*, 100.

matters. Her response to me was brief, pointed, firmly stated: "God's judgment matters more than my own."[4]

What does Advent mean to us? Maybe, it is just that. In the midst of all the commercials, advertisements, and all the cultural trappings, maybe it is just that. Like a distant, faint voice, that wakens us from a dream, echoing through the millenniums, from the wilderness of Judea into our lives in twenty-first century America: God's judgment matters more than our own.

As the pandemic roared on, I continued to think about God's judgement, not in the sense of fire and brimstone, but judgement as an opportunity of realignment.[5] How do I bring myself more in line with what God prioritizes? What have I learned about how out of whack my values were and are with God's during the pandemic? And how do I lead Main Street to make renewed commitments to seek ever more to become the beloved community that truly welcomes all? How do we move beyond simply talking the talk and actually walk the walk? Furthermore, what does John the Baptist's witness of living simply in a self-imposed exile say into my life? What does John's witness say to us American consumers who are devouring our world's resources at a frightening rate?

John who never knew high living would look at my lamentations of the inconveniences of the pandemic and say, "Oh please, just shut up already. Forget about Dylan. Have you ever listened to the song of the locusts?" And what would he say to all of us who have bemoaned the disruptions of retail supply that the pandemic wrought? Additionally, what would John think about all my institutional concerns about decline? Perhaps, he would denounce them all as idolatry. Perhaps, he would be the one to say, "Where, oh where, preacher man, is your faith?" I can only imagine the truth John would speak to the American Church about our preoccupations with expansive and expensive church campuses.

4. Coles, *Harvard Diary*, 101.

5. By no means am I drawing a correlation that the pandemic is God's judgment upon us. Viruses happen, and they have always happened. They are a part of the fabric of a broken and fallen world. How tragic were Billy Graham's comments that he made to an audience of 44,300 in Cooper Stadium in Columbus, Ohio in September 1993 when he proclaimed, "Is AIDS a judgment of God? I could not be sure, but I think so." After receiving tremendous backlash, Graham apologized for what he said. To contend that God creates viruses to punish humans for bad behavior reduces God to a cosmic sadist, a cruel divine dictator inflicting suffering on errant humans. Graham's statement was ill-conceived and added to the incredible pain of those already suffering from AIDS, and the pain of their loved ones. See Brammer, "Billy Graham leaves a painful legacy for LGBTQ people."

The middle of the month brought good news and a continuation of the bad. On December 14, Sandra Lindsay, an ICU nurse from Northwell Long Island Jewish Medical Center (NY) was the first American (non-trial) to receive the Pfizer/BioNTech COVID-19 vaccine. Upon hearing the news, I marveled at the lightning speed of the German pharmaceutical company to develop this wonder drug. Approximately, three quarters of a year after the American population truly became aware of this virus, and the vaccine is deployed.

The virus continued its deadly spread. By December 16, the death count had risen to 304,683. On March 16, 88 individuals were known to have died from COVID-19. Nine months later the cumulative loss now was equal to losing the entire population of the Arkansas cities of Little Rock, Fort Smith, and Clarksville. Gone, just like that. A week and a day later, the losses were equivalent to losing the additional cities of Dardanelle, Paris, and Hope. The death count by Christmas Eve was 327,173.

We had planned to have a 2 p.m. Christmas Eve parking lot service in addition to our livestream services, but the rain came down, and the parking lot service was cancelled. Sometimes, it seems like you cannot catch a break. We livestreamed the 4 p.m. Children's Christmas Eve service. During the 7 p.m. livestreamed traditional service, I was caught by surprise. Normally Christmas Eve services are full of hustle and bustle. But this year it was different. That night, I felt that I could time travel more unencumbered to the first century nativity. I experienced a palpable sense of God's presence. A minister friend said to me that he had pre-taped his Christmas Eve service, and it was the first time in thirty years that he was able to spend Christmas Eve at home. There were hidden blessings amidst the pandemic.

During the days that followed Christmas Eve, I pondered the oddness of it all. Another Christmas had come and gone, but this one, not easily forgotten, will be relived in stories told to our children and grandchildren. The narrations will begin, "Remember that Christmas Eve from so long ago that happened in the midst of the 2020 Pandemic . . . " This Christmas Eve made its mark in my memory as I stood in the pulpit preaching to an almost empty room. Whereas in years past the sanctuary was aglow with lit candles, this year just a few candles, held by those leading the service in music, song, and word, broke the darkness.

We did our best in the pandemic to make Christmas seem normal. We found ways to hold onto as many of the Christmas traditions as possible. We decorated our houses, baked goodies, hung up stockings for Santa to fill, sent out Christmas cards, and charged up our credit cards. We added to Jeff Bezos's wealth as UPS, USPS, and FedEx delivered all the packages we ordered on Amazon. We ventured with masks on into stores like Barnes & Noble, Wal Mart, Target, and Hanes Mall. But two aspects of the shopping expeditions were striking; the inventory was down, and the crowds were nowhere as densely packed as previous years.

We sang Christmas songs in the Church parking lot while sipping Hot Chocolate and Apple Cider. And if we are totally transparent, we also shed a tear missing activities that we hold dear, shed a tear for loved ones that we could not travel to see, and we shed a tear for loved ones that we have lost in the past year. Heavy on our hearts, as well, were all of those from our homelands and from around the world who died from COVID-19; God's children who would not be celebrating this holy season with their families. Empty chairs in living rooms decorated with Christmas trees and vacant spots at dining room tables became a new reality for far too many.

The lectionary text from the Gospel of Luke on Christmas Eve told how Joseph and Mary had to make a difficult journey that was made even more arduous as she was great with child. They traveled the rough roads from Nazareth in Galilee to Bethlehem in Judea. When the time arrived for the birth of their child, they found shelter in a stable, and Mary wrapped her first-born son in swaddling clothes and laid him in a manger.

Into this bleak night, born of danger and poverty, the miraculous manifested itself. An angel of the Lord appeared to the shepherds in the fields tending their flocks. The angel said, "Fear not, for behold, I bring you good news of great joy that will be for all the people. For unto you is born this day in the city of David a Savior, who is Christ the Lord."[6] Given directions by the angel, the shepherds went to see for themselves. When they found Mary, Joseph, and the baby, they told them all that the angel had said. They were amazed, and Mary treasured these things in her heart.

The savior born in a stable destabilizes and threatens the powers of this world. Love came down at Christmas, the old hymn proclaims. This is not a sentimental kind of love. It is a strong love, a robust love. A love that was there for those suffering in the first century harsh world of reversals, economic deprivations, capricious dictators, and ravaging diseases. It is a love that is there for us amid losses and gains, defeats and triumphs, and agonies and joys. It is a love that endures.

6. Luke 2: 10–11 (ESV).

The love that came down at Christmas is a love that perseveres and carries us through the storms of our world, pandemics, social turbulence, and troubles. It is a love that came into a broken world, seeking to heal our sometimes-shattered lives. The true spirit of Christmas does not rush past the pain of our world, or the pain of our lives: no Hallmark sentimentality, no plastic smiles, just an abiding presence that embraces our suffering. In C.S. Lewis's *The Last Battle*, Queen Lucy states, "In our world too, a stable once had something inside it that was bigger than our whole world."[7]

The headlines for the evening news on the last night of 2020 sounded all too familiar. Intensive Care Units across the nation were at capacity. The Center for Disease Control warned Americans not to congregate to celebrate the New Year. A new highly contagious strain that spread from the UK to the US has officials worried. In previous years, hundreds of thousands of people gathered in Times Square to watch the ball drop, but this year only a select will few have that privilege. More than 20 million cases of COVID-19 had been reported, and the death count exceeded 341,000. And despite the country being ravaged by the pandemic, President Trump continued his efforts to overturn the election results of one of the most secure elections in the history of the United States. I was beginning to think like the Methodist church the country was on its way to becoming the *Untied States*.

On New Year's Eve, Rhonda and I fought to stay awake to welcome in the New Year. We were more than glad to say adieu to 2020. The countdown began. The moment arrived, a New Year and *Auld Lang Syne* played. But we did not know it. Despite our valiant efforts, we were asleep on the couch. Five days later, January 6 (Wednesday), was the Feast Day of Epiphany.

Wednesday mornings are my sermon preparation time. That morning of every week, I work in my home office. On January 6, I was revisiting the first chapter of Mark's Gospel, digging into William Lane's commentary, and wondering, "What could I say about John the Baptist that I had not already said on December 6?" As noon approached, I went into the kitchen to make a cup of coffee and to find something to cook in the microwave for my midday meal. Settling into the den with my tray of coffee and nuked lunch, I turned on news and watched Trump make a speech that many Republicans wished that he had never made. It was a crossing of the Rubicon. There were the policy accomplishments that conservative Republicans could point to prior to that defining moment. Then there was January 6.

7. Lewis, *The Last Battle*, 161.

Trump was not the first speaker in the lineup for the *Save America Rally*. Trump's sons Eric and Donald Jr. had already spoken as well as Rudy Giuliani, the man once regarded as America's mayor.

I did not see any of those speeches. I also missed part of the President's speech, but I heard him continue to harangue about how the most secure election in this nation's history was riddled with fraud and that the election was not only stolen from him but also stolen from all of his supporters. A massive crowd turned out that day, and Trump was throwing red meat to starving lions. It was an incendiary oration that lasted approximately an hour. I had never watched an American President engage in such vitriolic rhetoric in my life. Furthermore, he kept calling on Vice President Mike Pence to throw away the legitimate election and create a coup. It was as if Trump confused the United States of America with a banana republic.

Trump said, "You don't concede when there's theft involved." The President told the massive, agitated crowd, "You have to show strength and you have to be strong." He then invited the protestors to walk down Pennsylvania Avenue to the Capitol. At 1 p.m. lawmakers gathered in the House of Representatives Chamber for a joint session of Congress to count the votes of the Electoral College. Normally, that was a ceremonial moment, but the world and American citizens watched in horror as the events unfolded. At 1:15 p.m., the rioters began struggling with the police and by 2:11 p.m., the insurrectionists had breached police lines. They scaled down the Capitol. Storming into the building, they broke glass, overpowered Police Officers, and paraded through the rotunda carrying Trump and Confederate flags. As they looted and vandalized, they also paused for photos which many of them posted on social media as if they had made their nation proud, as if they were the new George Washington's throwing off the yoke of the oppressors. I was stupefied and horrified as I watched the events unfold, and I wondered how did we as a nation arrive at this destination of watching mayhem in the seat of our national government? We were left to wonder if our great union would hold.

The insurrections had taken the Capitol. The lawmakers were evacuated. At 4:17 p.m., Trump released a video in which he said to the mob of rioters, looters, and criminals, "Go home. We love you. You are very special people." At 5:40 p.m., it was announced that the Capitol had been retaken and was now secure. At 8 p.m., the session of Congress resumed. Mitt Romney, the Republican Senator from Utah who knows firsthand the pain of losing a presidential election took to the floor and made no bones about it: "Now we gather due to a selfish man's injured pride . . . What happened here today was an insurrection incited by the President of the United States." The lawmakers continued their work and at 3:33 a.m., Joe Biden had the necessary electoral vote count of 270 to secure the election as the next President. I stayed awake watching it until the joint session ended on January 7 at 3:44 a.m.

I wrote an article for the twelfth of January edition of *The Kernersville News*. There was no way not to acknowledge the elephant in the room.

Last Wednesday, January 6, Christians, from all over the world and here in the United States, marked the Feast Day of Epiphany. It is a day when Christians celebrate the light of Christ entering into our dark world; God's Word made flesh for people of all ages, nations, races, and genders. In other words, when it comes to God's grace, all means all. It is also a day that we commemorate the Magi's visit to the Christ child bringing gifts of gold, frankincense, and myrrh. The Magi were non-Jewish. They were Persians. Epiphany lauds, as well, the revelation of Christ to the Gentiles.

When King Herod the Great heard about the Wise Men from the East, who traveled a long, difficult journey, following a star, seeking to pay homage to the newborn king of the Jews, he became frightened. Secretly, he called for the Wise Men to appear before him, and he learned from them the exact time of the star's appearance. He sent them on to Bethlehem with the instruction that when they find the child, they should report back to him so that he could also go and pay this new king adulation. Herod had no intention of paying respect but wanted to put an end to any threats to his reign.

The Roman Senate named Herod the king of Judea. When he became king, he went after the Sanhedrin, the Supreme Court, and gutted it of its political power. He ordered the death of many of its members. He also had three hundred court officials killed. He guarded his power and his kingdom closely and had a personal bodyguard of more than two thousand soldiers.

Herod eliminated all threats to his throne including ordering the executions of his wife Mariamne, and his sons Aristabulus, Alexander, and Antipater. The Roman Emperor Augustus said, "It was safer to be Herod's pig than Herod's son." In addition, he had his mother-in-law, brother-in-law, and grandfather-in-law killed. He also gave orders that Jerusalem's most distinguished citizens be arrested on false charges and imprisoned so that when he died, they would be killed. He knew that no one would mourn his death. He wanted to ensure that when he died, tears would flow.

Dictators, the world is full of dictators and wannabe dictators. It always has been. It is a tale as old as time. Having traveled through communist East Germany, Czechoslovakia, and having stood in the conference building in the DMZ looking out the window into North Korea, I know, for sure, that I do not want to live in a land where the Herods of the world rule. I am so grateful that I live in a democracy.

The Wise Men were warned in a dream not to return to Herod and tell him the whereabouts of this newborn child born to be the King of Kings. And fortunately, for us, they listened.

As we celebrated the Feast of Epiphany in the cathedral of our hearts, darkness descended upon our nation's capital as rioters and thugs desecrated the Temple of Democracy, the People's House, where the U.S. Senate and House of Representatives debate and make decisions that affect our lives.

We were shocked as we witnessed the images of mob violence, of looters, vandals, breaking windows, overrunning the Capital Police, ransacking offices, and parading through the entire building. Tragically, at least five people have died as a result of the riot. Wednesday will long live in our memories. Glued to the news, I stayed up late in the night and early into the morning hours watching the House and the Senate count the electoral votes. Though the rioters attempted to disrupt and thwart the democratic process, democracy did not crumble, and the will of the people prevailed. This is a great country, and I know that we will get through this storm as previous generations have weathered and navigated so many other storms. Democracy can, if protected, triumph over dictators of despair, and over architects of anarchy and tyranny.

As people of faith, as people of hope, we wonder, how do we respond and hold true to who we are as followers of Christ, as followers of the One who stopped his own disciples from creating an insurrection? As followers of the One who said to Peter, "Put your sword back in its place for all who draw the sword will die by the sword."[8] Christ reached out his hand and healed Malchus's ear.[9] We do not follow in the footsteps of those who sow discord, strife, fear, hatred, and violence. We eschew those who seek to rob others of their dignity as children of God. We follow in the footsteps of the One who brought healing and hope to broken and desperate people.

As a people of faith, we are called to work for justice and peace. The prophet Micah declared, "He has told you, O mortal,

8. Matthew 26:52 (NIV).
9. John 18:10–11.

115

what is good; and what does the Lord require of you but to do jus-
tice, and to love kindness, and to walk humbly with your God?"[10]
May we, as individuals and as a nation, seek to be the people that
God calls us to be.

On January 13, the House of Representatives impeached President
Trump a second time by a vote of 237 to 197. Four Congresspersons ab-
stained, and ten Republicans voted to impeach. Trump went down in history as the only President to be impeached twice, and the only President to
lose the national vote twice. January was the month of the three I's: Insurrection, Impeachment, and the Inauguration of Joe Biden as the forty-sixth
President of the United States.

The Church Council met on January 28. A motion was presented by
the Worship Committee to reopen for in-person worship (continuing of
course with livestream) on the first Sunday in Lent, February 21. The motion passed.

On January 31, 2021, the news reported on a major winter storm that
had already blanketed the Midwest in snow and was heading toward the
northeast. The reporter said that more than 100 million people would be
affected by the storm, and the blizzard is expected to affect eleven states. A
new national mask mandate went into effect for public transportation. A
warning was made about new highly transmissible variants of the virus that
will lead to a surge potentially unlike anything that we have seen thus far.
Vaccine distribution problems will be compounded by the incoming winter
storm. Anti-Putin protests rock Russia. And more than 440,000 Americans
have died from COVID-19. A year and three days prior, President Trump
had been warned how potentially deadly this new virus would be. On
February 2, 2020, Trump said to Sean Hannity of Fox News that we have
"pretty much shut it down coming in from China."[11]

---

10. Micah 6:8 (NRSV).

11. Woodward, *Rage*, xvii.

Chapter 12

The Days of Discontent

On the first day in February (2021), John called us to let us know that he had received a job offer from a hospital in Odessa, Texas. His hope of moving back to the South was materializing, but I did not expect it to be that far southwest. Yet, I was grateful that doors were opening for him. After wrapping up his life in Wrightstown, he said that he planned to spend ten days with us before heading to the Lone Star state.

On the first Sunday of February, we were still closed to in-person worship. We celebrated and partook of the Eucharist as a community from a distance. From the beginning of the pandemic, I was uncomfortable with virtual Communion, even though Bishop Leeland gave a dispensation to the clergy authorizing remote Eucharistic practices until the pandemic concluded. As one who had served as an altar server from second grade until twelfth grade, ringing the bell as the host and chalice were elevated, and holding the golden paten under each chin lest the *Corpus Christi* fall to the floor and accidentally be trampled on, Communion has always held a special place in my heart. Word and Table never should have been separated. Though I missed the intimacy of beholding the eyes of the ones who came forward to receive the body and blood of Christ, I knew my bishop was right. In times of crisis, the church must respond and find new ways to meet the needs of the present age.

It was a Eucharistic crisis that led to the final determination that Methodism would not remain as a renewal movement within the Anglican

Church as the Franciscans had remained as a renewal movement within the Roman Catholic Church. After the Revolutionary War, many Anglican clergy departed America, returning to England, resulting in a clergy shortage. When the Bishop of London refused in 1784 to ordain a Methodist minister for the United States, John Wesley (an Anglican priest) took matters into his own hands, literally, by consecrating another Anglican priest (Thomas Coke) as a superintendent for America. Coke would cross the Atlantic and, in the Christmas Conference of 1784 in Baltimore, ordain deacons and presbyters. Wesley determined that Coke and Francis Asbury would be co-superintendents of America and at that same conference, Coke consecrated Asbury as a bishop. Thus Wesley, due to the crisis of American Methodists not being able to receive the sacrament of the Lord's altar, made a way, departing from the tradition of his own Anglican church that only bishops could ordain prospective clergy. [1]

Centuries later, in Kernersville, that Sunday evening (February 7), Rhonda and I watched the Tampa Bay Buccaneers defeat the Kansas City Chiefs by a score of 31–9, and receive the Vince Lombardi trophy for Superbowl LV. Tom Brady, the forty-three-year-old quarterback, secured his seventh Super Bowl victory. On Tuesday of that same week, six Republican senators voted that the second impeachment trial of President Trump was constitutional.

The next evening was Ash Wednesday, and the service was virtual. Prior to the event, people stopped by the church to pick up their worship supplies for the service. Those who gathered that evening with family and friends had someone to make the mark of the cross on their foreheads while they heard the words, "Remember that you are dust and to dust you shall return." Those who were alone had to paint the cross on themselves with the mixture of oil and ash. As the cross was traced on my forehead, I meditated on the ancient words that were spoken. They possessed added gravity in the midst of a pandemic.

Late that same night, John arrived home after a long drive from Wrightstown to Kernersville. We talked for a while and then turned in. It was great to have him home and to help plan his transition to Texas. On Saturday, while watching the news we learned that the Senate had voted 57–43 in favor of impeaching Donald Trump on the charge of inciting an

---

1. There is debate as to whether John Wesley secured apostolic succession from the Greek Orthodox Bishop Erasmus of Arcadia. Some contend that Erasmus consecrated Wesley as a bishop.

insurrection, but the vote fell short of the two-thirds majority that is required. The next day was Transfiguration Sunday, and I reflected on just how much had changed since Transfiguration Sunday 2019.

John left for Texas on the twentieth. We had been watching the news that week, learning what we could about the snow and ice storm that had hit Texas. There was a widespread loss of electricity, and many did not have heat for their homes. The news also reported on any number of vehicle wrecks with cars and trucks colliding into one another and others sliding off the road. We worried for John all that day. When he got to Sulphur Springs, Texas, we received a phone call. He had tried to get a room at the LaQuinta, but they were full of not only travelers but also of families who had no heat in their homes. He got a room in the Hampton Inn and made his way to Odessa on the twenty-first.

The Commission on the General Conference met on the twentieth and decided that the next in-person General Conference would meet in Minneapolis from August 29 to September 6, 2022. The separation protocol will have to wait for now. Before the pandemic became real, I wondered if the time had come for the warring factions in the United Methodist Church to bless each other and go their separate ways. As the pandemic lingered, my position changed. If I were the Pope of the United Methodist Church, I would speak from the chair mandating that we hold the denomination together. In addition, I would also issue the proclamation that every local church can determine who can be married in its sanctuary. I would include in my papal document that every annual conference can also determine who can be ordained.

Last time I checked, no conclave had met, no white smoke had poured forth from the chimney, and I remain one of many, many Elders in United Methodism. I am not even one of the 862 delegates that will gather for General Conference in 2022 (if indeed that even happens). With a third of the delegates coming from Africa, with the rise of the Delta variant, and with the low vaccine rate in Africa, I would not be surprised if General Conference is postponed yet again.

I believe that together is better than separation or fragmentation. Some of my closest friends are evangelical United Methodist pastors. I do not want to think of a day when we are in separate denominations. I grieve that reality. But what will be will be, and many of my friends will align with the Global Methodist Church. Yet amid all of that separation, we remain brothers and sisters in Christ. Though I would mandate that the denomination hold together, I realize I am an idealist, and when the General Conference finally does meet, some allowance for a gracious exit will most certainly be made for members of the Wesleyan Covenant Association and possibly as well for those on the far left.

On the first Sunday in Lent (February 21), Main Street UMC held its first in-person worship service since having closed before the first Sunday in December. Strict social procedures were followed. On February 22, the number of Americans who had died from COVID-19 had now crossed the half-a-million mark. On February 28, Rhonda and I met some friends for lunch at Outwest Steak House in Kernersville. While enjoying the meal and the fellowship, it dawned on me that Rhonda and I had not eaten inside a restaurant since we had had brunch with John at Kitchen 87 in Mount Holly, New Jersey, on March 14, 2020. I could hardly believe it—fifty weeks without dining in-person in a restaurant—fifty weeks without attending any in-person concerts, or movies at the theatre—fifty weeks without traveling outside the state of North Carolina, and many months not even outside of Forsyth County.

On the news that evening, the CDC approved a new vaccine by Johnson & Johnson. More good news was reported, with a declining number of people hospitalized and more than 48 million Americans now having received at least one dose of a COVID vaccine. Tragically, by this point in the pandemic the United States had already exceeded half-a million deaths. The estimated deaths for the world was 2.5 million. Unfortunately, the USA was winning a prize that no one wanted.

Breaking with the etiquette of previous presidents, Trump attacked President Biden at the Conservative Political Action Committee (CPAC) claiming that Biden presided over the most disastrous first month of any American President. The former President also contended that Biden had sold out America's children to the Teachers' Union. Trump also continued his long egregious claim that the election had been rigged and that the Supreme Court and the other courts had refused to do anything about it. Approximately six weeks after the inauguration of a new president, the former president is still seeking to undermine his successor and democracy itself. He continued to demonstrate that he possesses no interest in helping the nation heal from a divisive election.

Other news stories of the day included another woman who came forward claiming that Governor Andrew Cuomo of New York had sexually harassed her. Pro-democracy demonstrators in Myanmar were met by the police who killed eighteen demonstrators. High above all the troubles of our planet, two NASA astronauts completed a spacewalk. On March 1, the Wesley Covenant Association unveiled the logo and plans for the new Global Methodist Church.

Rhonda and I took a staycation from the eighth to the fourteenth of March and caught up on projects around the house. For the most part we remained in Kernersville, but on the tenth we indulged in a day trip to Blowing Rock and Boone. Our second in-person meal occurred that day at Lost Province in downtown Boone. On the fifteenth, the security forces in Myanmar killed at least thirty-eight people. As the days passed, more protests erupted around the world: Lebanon, Turkey, and England. The days of discontent continued. The Myanmar military killed one hundred and fourteen protestors on March 27. I was haunted by Jesus's words, "And you will hear of wars and rumors of wars; see that you are not alarmed; for this must take place, but the end is not yet."[2] The end may not yet be, but we sometimes wonder just how much more our hearts can take.

The Gospel passage for Palm Sunday (March 28) was Mark 11: 1–11. As they were approaching Jerusalem, Jesus sent two of his disciples into the nearby village to secure a colt that had never been ridden. "As you enter the village," he instructed them, "you will find the colt tied there. If anyone asks you all why you are taking it, just tell them that the Lord needs it, and the colt will be returned shortly." Obviously, Jesus had prearranged the loan of the colt for a specific function that he had in mind.

The disciples brought back the colt and threw their cloaks on it, and Jesus sat on it. The prophet Zechariah proclaimed, "Rejoice greatly, O daughter Zion! Shout aloud, O daughter Jerusalem! Lo, your king comes to you; triumphant and victorious is he, humble and riding on a donkey, on a colt, the foal of a donkey."[3] People spread their cloaks on the road and palm branches as well. The palm branch had been a symbol of Jewish Nationalism since 167 BC when the Maccabees revolted against the Greek occupation of Judea. Spreading the cloaks and branches on the road, they cried out, "Hosanna! Blessed is the one who comes in the name of the Lord! Blessed is the coming kingdom of our ancestor David! Hosanna in the highest heaven!"[4]

2. Matthew 24:6 (NRSV).

3. Zechariah 9:9 (NRSV).

4. Mark 11:9b, 10 (NRSV).

"The coming kingdom of our ancestor David" was not idle talk. First century Judea was full of social and political turmoil. There were the zealots, referred to by many as terrorists, who had no qualms about utilizing violence to achieve political aims. On the other end of the spectrum were those who were prospering during a foreign occupation, the elite who had accommodated themselves to Roman rule. Rulers and leaders like Herod Antipas, the Chief Priests, Pilate, and the commanders of the occupying Roman military all had vested interest in maintaining the existing social order. Yet, in the midst of all the political intrigue, you also had the common people, people of the land, suffering under unfair taxation, economic exploitation, desperate poverty, illiteracy, and government violence routinely used against any who threaten the status quo. Then there were the Essenes, who thought that society was far too corrupt for their participation, and they withdrew to the wilderness to live a monastic life.

The people that day on Palm Sunday were not expecting or hoping for a crucified Lord. They were anticipating a new King to bring the glories of Israel of old. Wave those symbols of Jewish nationalism in the air! Lay them down on the ground before our new King! What is clear in the passage is that Jesus was staging not just a religious parade but also a political demonstration. People say, "You should keep politics out of the church." My response is, "It would be a lot easier to do so if Jesus had not been so insistent on inserting politics into the Gospel."

According to Marcus Borg and John Dominic Crossan, Jesus staged on Palm Sunday a political counterdemonstration. In their book *The Last Week*, Borg and Crossan, two New Testament scholars, stated that Jesus rode into Jerusalem on Palm Sunday, coming in from the east on a donkey, a symbol of peace, surrounded by hurting and oppressed people, who were hoping that he could end their suffering. And from the west, Pontius Pilate, escorted by imperial soldiers and cavalry headed into the city from Caesarea Maritima to maintain the order during the Passover festival that would see the population of Jerusalem greatly increase.[5] During the Passover festival, people would remember the story of how God liberated their ancestors from the tyranny of another empire, of a Pharaoh and all his many chariots, riders, and foot soldiers. The hearts of those at the Passover festival hoped against hope that God would do it again, that God would work another miracle of deliverance.

5. Borg and Crossan, *The Last Week*, 2–5.

Two parades reflecting two very different kingdoms. One, where the Master lays down his life for his servants, and the other where Caesar and his representatives create rivers of suffering. Two very different kingdoms: The Kingdom of God versus a dictatorship. Jesus and Pontius Pilate, squaring off on Good Friday. Pilate will go to bed that night thinking he has won the day.

Can you see the faces of the crowd that Palm Sunday? Faces of people who had been personally touched by Jesus, perhaps he had healed them of their infirmities, perhaps they had eaten the fish and bread he provided by the seashore. And other faces, exhausted faces, hoping for a new day when the yoke of Rome would be thrown off. Faces trying to find hope amid all their hurts and disappointments. Faces of people who looked to Jesus to restore their broken spirits, give them courage to gather the shards of their shattered dreams, and start dreaming again. Here is our Messiah who will build his earthly kingdom and bring about a new age. Two millenniums later, and the church still struggles with the temptations of politicians, preachers, and evangelists who claim that they can usher in a new religious and political kingdom, promising to deliver us and society from all that ails us.

Monday and Tuesday of our Holy Week came and went. On Wednesday, after the Oasis service, I went home and watched the evening news. It was the last day of March. The headline stories of the day included: Day three of the Derek Chauvin murder trial in Minneapolis. Videos shown in court were from the officer's body cam and from store surveillance. The clerk, who noticed the fake twenty-dollar bill that George Floyd had used, wished that he had never flagged it, that he had never brought it to the attention of the manager. He wished that he had just taken it and then paid the store back out of his own monies so that Floyd would not have died. An elderly African American man sobbed on the witness stand as he recounted the trauma that he had incurred while watching Floyd suffocate. He testified that he had yelled to Floyd, telling him to settle down and not resist, that you cannot win when you are in a confrontation with the police.

Also making the news that day was an announcement from France of a month-long lockdown due to a COVID-19 outbreak. In the United States, more than 95 million have received at least one dose of the vaccine. But nationwide infections are up 17.5 percent. A new wave is threatening. As the reporter continued talking about the challenges of the pandemic, I wondered, how much longer would it last? I had lost confidence that things would get back anytime soon to the way there were before the pandemic, and I began to wonder if the pandemic in one form or another would last another year. How many additional variants are yet to be discovered in a nation that has long struggled to define and understand individual freedom versus collective freedom? How many more waves will come crashing in upon us? A year later and the storm seems nowhere close to being over; a year later and more than 551,000 have died.

The news also reported that an arrest had been made in the case of a malicious attack on a 65-year-old Asian woman. On Monday, a man yelling anti-Asian rhetoric shouted at the woman that she did not belong in the United States. He assaulted her on a Manhattan Street, first kicking her in the stomach and then when she fell, stomping on her head multiple times. The reporter also stated that the spectators who witnessed the assault did not intervene or call 911 in the midst of the violent attack.

After turning off the news, I retreated to my home office and sat in my chair and pondered what a year and two weeks it had been. Tomorrow is Maundy Thursday, and we will gather in the sanctuary and remember that night that was unlike any other night in the lives of the apostles—that night when Jesus said to his apostles, "Do not let your hearts be troubled"—that night when he took the bread, blessed it, broke it, and gave it to them saying, "Take, eat, this is my body given to you"—that night when he took the chalice and said, "Drink of this all of you, this is my blood poured out for you." If only the Apostles had known what was about to break forth into their lives, their hearts surely would have known no shortage of trouble. As it was, they traveled from the Upper Room in Jerusalem through the Kidron Valley arriving in the Garden of Gethsemane. There Jesus would sweat blood. There Jesus would ask Father God if the cup might be removed. There Jesus would be betrayed for thirty pieces of silver.

All four Gospels identify Judas (one of the twelve chosen apostles) as the person who betrayed Jesus. Matthew is the only Gospel that reveals what happened to Judas after the betrayal. In the Acts of the Apostles, Luke tells the story differently from Matthew. Acts 1:18 states that Judas bought a field with the money he had received and fell headlong into that field, bursting open, and his bowels gushed out. Matthew wrote that when Judas saw that Jesus was condemned, Judas repented, and returned the thirty pieces of silver to the chief priests and elders, throwing the coins down on the Temple floor. Feeling remorse, despondent, Judas went out and hanged himself. Frederick Buechner contends that Matthew's portrait makes better psychological sense.[6]

There have been many reasons given on why Judas betrayed Jesus. One of those, the obvious one, is that Judas betrayed Jesus for thirty pieces of silver. That never seemed that compelling to me. First of all, thirty pieces of silver is not like winning the Powerball Lottery. And if Matthew recorded the story correctly, Judas returned the money after the plan unraveled. Another thought is that Judas was angry because Jesus did not usher in the new Davidic kingdom. Judas became disillusioned, realizing that Jesus was not the promised Messiah, but just another compelling, miracle-working rabbi. Judas's anger and disillusionment festered until it busted forth into action. The reason that I find compelling contends that Judas remained a true believer in Jesus. He was just giving Jesus a significant push to help bring in the new messianic age, an earthly kingdom. Judas orchestrated the forcing of Jesus's hand so the Nazarene rabbi would no longer plod along but bring in the new kingdom with haste. Judas never expected Jesus to end up on a cross.

"Can Judas be forgiven?" is a question I have been asked before. Jesus states, "woe to that one by whom the Son of Man is betrayed! It would have been better for that one not to have been born."[7] But that does not equate to betrayal being an unforgiveable sin. When I am asked the question of whether Judas can be forgiven or not, I quickly respond, "That's way above my pay grade." On the morning of crucifixion Friday, when he beheld that his plan had gone awry, Judas repented. His mode of death does not negate the sincerity of his repentance. Only God knows the human heart, and final judgement belongs to God.

The late Robert Siegel, a renowned poet and author of children's literature, was giving a guest lecture to an English class. I do not remember what that lecture was about. But I do remember and will never forget a story he shared that day. He said Jesus and the apostles and other disciples are feasting away in the Messianic Banquet. They are laughing, partaking of a great meal, and celebrating together. A few feet away from the front of the table where they are all gathered is an endless dark hole. After they have feasted for a thousand years, Jesus looks down and sees an arm emerge from the darkness, and then a leg, and finally a person rolls out of that hideous pit

6. Buechner, *Peculiar Treasures*, 93.
7. Matthew 26:24b (NRSV).

onto the floor. Jesus looks down and with a loving smile, says, "Judas, what took you so long?"

I do not remember where Siegel got that story; I just remember the impact that it made. God's amazing grace is bigger than I could ever imagine, and I suspect that that same awesome grace is big enough to make space for even the Apostle Judas. C.S. Lewis wrote, "The hardness of God is kinder than the softness of men, and His compulsion is our liberation."[8]

8. Lewis, *Surprised by Joy*, 229.

Epilogue

Hopes and Prayers

The first Sunday in March 2020, we feasted on bread and grape juice, embraced each other, shook hands, sang with gusto, and never gave a thought to social distancing. On the second Sunday, we refrained from handshakes and hugging, but we still packed into the fellowship hall to hear the Assistant to the Bishop brief us on *The Protocol of Reconciliation and Grace through Separation*. By the third Sunday, we who had never livestreamed a service before were now in the broadcast business. Granted NBC was not calling us for tips and suggestions, but still our services were live TV and available to all with an internet connection.

Time passed. The days turned into weeks, and the weeks into months, and the COVID-19 death count grew in ways that we never could have imagined. During the pandemic, we who were so used to having hamburgers and life our way all of a sudden met a storm that ran its own course despite our best efforts to control and manage. We became frustrated that neither science nor the government could provide us with the solution that would transport us to how we lived life before the pandemic fell upon us like a curtain at closing time.

As the months passed, even more storms erupted on our city streets: protests over George Floyd's horrific death, over police violence, over racism, over economic injustice, and during those protests, bad actors did what bad actors do and engaged in violence, looting, and vandalism. Solomon, the wise old king, wrote that there is nothing new under the sun.[1] Fires broke out in America figuratively and literally.

Amid all that pain, chaos, trauma, and violence, the political leadership of our nation could not come together and lead us in feeding our good angels and not the bad ones. The United States and the United Methodist Church have a lot in common. They are nowhere as united as we would hope. The divisions in both are deep and were present before the pandemic began.

Canyons of division are such a part of the USA and the UMC. Maybe the dividing line is human sexuality, or socio-economic groupings, or a charismatic politician, or gender, or race, but whatever the lines are that divide us, the Gospel calls us to remember that we follow in the footsteps of the one who welcomed sinners and broke bread in the house of the despised. We follow in the path of the one who challenged us to ask, "Just who is my neighbor?" We follow in the footsteps of the one who broke down national and ethnic barriers. We follow in the way of the one who confronted the political powers of the world and the religious establishment. And for that he ended up on the cross and said, "Oh, by the way, follow me there too."

It was the summer of 1982, and I was on a train bound for somewhere—Paris, Amsterdam, Rome—I do not remember, but carved into my memory like stone is how the conversation began. In a train compartment across from me sat a Roman Catholic priest. He was an old man, but, of course, back then I thought sixty was ancient.

In my hands, I held open Dietrich Bonhoeffer's *The Cost of Discipleship*. It was first published in 1937 in German entitled *Nachfolge*, which means "following." I, a Biblical Studies major at a liberal arts Christian college in Springfield, Missouri, found Bonhoeffer's thought riveting. Arrested by the Nazis April 5, 1943, he was executed on April 9, 1945, one of the Flossenbürg martyrs.

Engrossed reading the book, I did not, at first, note how the priest stared at the cover. But I could not help but notice when he pointed at it and spoke to me in German. He knew only a few words in English, and I knew even fewer words in German. Language divided us. But with the help of another train passenger, a woman, who knew a few more words in English but not that many more, his story began to unfold.

During the Second World War, he had served in the German Army. Captured by the Russians, he spent time in a concentration camp. At the

1. Ecclesiastes 1:9.

128

hands of the Communists, he suffered greatly for his faith. Bonhoeffer's thought, theology, and life became a treasure trove to this priest because he too, from a different vantage point had lived it.

As I looked in his wearied but joyful pale blue eyes, I reflected on my good fortune: how I never witnessed friends die in battle, how my days were not spent looking through barbed wire hearing a foreign tongue bark out orders intending to humiliate, and how I had never been beaten for my faith or starved. As I regarded him, I knew his eyes had seen far too much of human cruelty, violence, and capriciousness. Yet, he wore the collar, representing the hope that there is a power beyond the insanity of this world, bearing witness that one day justice will roll down like ever-flowing waters.

Two people, one old and one young, a German and an American, spellbound by the vision of a Lutheran pastor theologian who many years before wrote, "When Christ calls a man, he bids him come and die."[2] Before we parted, the old priest gave me a holy card, Raphael's portrait of the Trinity—Father, Son and Holy Ghost—complete with angels and Mary. And it is still in the book I held so long ago on the train, a book that I pull off the shelf often letting it prophetically speak into my life.

Dietrich Bonhoeffer was greatly impacted by the writings of Karl Barth. In time they became friends and compatriots in the struggle against National Socialism. One of Barth's sayings gives me comfort in such a time as this: "To fold one's hands in prayer is the beginning of an uprising against the disorder of the world."[3] I remember Frederick Herzog, who was a former assistant and student of Karl Barth, sharing with me what an East German soldier had said about the demonstrators who facilitated the social unrest that helped bring about the downfall of the totalitarian regime in East Germany. Herzog and I had already been talking for some time in his office. He was gracious with his time. As I stood up to leave, he followed me to the doorway, and his face was almost aglow as he quoted the East German soldier who said, "We were trained to be ready for everything except when they came at us with candles and prayers."

In so many ways, my work here is a long lament about the pandemic, the decline of the Church, the divisive political climate that sacrifices the public good for winning elections, the social storms, our country's ever-present struggle with race, and the continued warring factions within the church and the nation. But the error one can easily make when overwhelmed

2. Bonhoeffer, *The Cost of Discipleship*, 99.

3. Lochman, *The Lord's Prayer in Our Time*, 18–19.

with the struggles of this age is to believe that somehow our age is more challenging than previous ages.

There are no easy solutions to any of these problems that have been lifted up, yet my hope remains. My hope remains that God will have a church. Perhaps, the church will not look like it is currently configured, but God will have a church. And perhaps change is not all bad. Maybe, we have all been somewhat guilty of religious institutional idolatry. My hope is found in saints like that old priest on the train whose name I forgot so long ago but is remembered by God, someone who continued to exude the joy of the Lord despite all the heartbreak that he had endured. My hope is found in the church that produces ordinary saints who often are the glue of their communities. More times than not, their names have been lost to history, but their lived lives were the leaven in the bread.

Those of us who serve the institutional church can sometimes get lost in the bricks, the mortar, the budget, the building campaign, and the worship and membership numbers. Reinhold Niebuhr was introduced to a business club "as a pastor who had recently built a new church at 'the impressive cost of $170,000.'"[4] It was 1921 and that was a significant amount of money. Niebuhr was approximately twenty-nine years old. As he meditated upon that moment, he thought that his church council would have gotten a good laugh, knowing as they did how little he had done in generating the monies necessary for building the structure. I resonated with Niebuhr on that. But it was natural enough for businessmen to celebrate what was valued in their work world.

Niebuhr then wrote about a twenty-fifth anniversary celebration of a friend's pastorate. The toastmaster celebrated the pastor's successful ministry by listing that under his tenure "the congregation had 'doubled its membership, installed a new organ, built a parsonage, decorated the church and wiped out its debt.'"[5] One wonders if Barbara Brown Taylor left the local church hoping to avoid the day when that speech would be made as a summation of her ministry. Niebuhr dryly commented that nothing was spoken about the pastor's words of comfort that he gave to aching hearts, and not a word about the pastor's inspiration that he provided to "thirsting souls."[6] Niebuhr then makes an observation pointed at us in the Methodist tradition: "Let us be thankful that there is no quarterly meeting in our

4. Niebuhr, *Leaves from the Notebook of a Tamed Cynic*, 31.

5. Niebuhr, *Leaves from the Notebook of a Tamed Cynic*, 31, 32.

6. Niebuhr, *Leaves from the Notebook of a Tamed Cynic*, 32.

denomination and no need of giving a district superintendent a bunch of statistics to prove that our ministry is successful."[7]

How easy it is to get lost in new and old buildings, budgets, statistics, church growth and church decline (two sides of the same coin), and whether the denomination will split or not. I left one denomination before and have no plans on leaving another. I left that denomination because it excluded my father from receiving the Eucharist because he was divorced. His church (the Roman Catholic Church) could not make space for "sinners" like him but had no trouble allowing predatory priests to preside over, partake, and distribute the Eucharist.[8] Sometimes bishops and lawyers lose their souls fighting to preserve that which corrodes. My hope is not found in them, nor is it found in people who use the exclusion, alienation, and condemnation of others as a rallying call to build a kingdom.

My ultimate hope is in the Lord of the Resurrection, and the community that he founded that continues on through the ages, regardless of the denominational names that are emblazoned on church signs and letterheads. My hope is found in people like Sister Theresa and Sister Coletta who picked the flowers from their own garden to ensure that every Sunday morning there were floral arrangements on the altar at Saint Scholastica's Catholic Church in Shoal Creek, Arkansas. My hope is found in the community of Christ as it serves others. My hope is found in my local church as my laity continually give of themselves serving in feeding programs for the hungry, handing out food to any who need it, going on mission trips, helping others, and being the hands and feet of Christ. That is where my hope resides, in the church doing the work of God's kingdom in the here and now.

7. Niebuhr, *Leaves from the Notebook of a Tamed Cynic*, 32.

8. The film *Spotlight* powerfully tells the story of *The Boston Globe* reporters who investigated the cover-up by the church hierarchy of the sexual abuse of children.

6-Week Small Group Discussion Guide

By Joe A. Hamby

WEEK 1: READ THE PREFACE, CHAPTERS 1 & 2

1. In his preface, Mike offers this prophetic word:

   The church two or three generations from now may not have sala-ried clergy, staff, or other professionals, nor will it necessarily have buildings. The church, in previous ages, has prospered in just such circumstances. Perhaps God is leading us into an iconoclastic age where institutional idols are deconstructed. The decline of the church may very well be leading us into rediscovering the Gospel.

   - In what ways can our buildings become an idol we worship in place of God?
   - Can you imagine a church without buildings? How might we be-come a stronger church without buildings?
   - How might a church without salaried clergy or staff lead us into rediscovering the Gospel?

2. In chapter one, Mike describes the post-Covid world we entered in 2020:

By the first Sunday in October, so much had changed. So many aspects of worship we once took for granted were gone; masks were mandatory, temperatures were taken before entering the narthex, and everyone provided contact information. Ushers directed people to socially distanced seating; people who had occupied the same pew with their friends for decades were dislocated. No congregational singing was allowed and no handshakes, hugs, or kisses before or after the service.

- What do you miss about pre-pandemic church? Are there things you do not miss?

3. Mike describes what a disciple of Jesus will experience in one foreboding sentence: *"Jesus forecast storms, rock strewn roads, and dangers from religious and political powers that the disciples would experience if they kept following him."*

   - Mike's understanding of the disciple's path aligns with activist Shane Claiborne's claims in his book *The Irresistible Revolution*: *"So if the world hates us, we take courage that it hated Jesus first. If you're wondering whether you'll be safe, just look at what they did to Jesus and those who followed him. There are safer ways to live than by being a Christian."* Why would Mike and Shane consider Christianity unsafe?
   - How do religious powers present a danger to Jesus's disciples today?

4. Commenting on the schism in Methodism, Mike argues that the issue of homosexuality has eclipsed other equally important concerns:

   Why this issue? How does this one issue, with all the many problems of America and the world, rise to the top, supplanting all others? Why is homosexuality the issue that generates heated responses? Methodists are relatively quiet over a host of other issues: economic injustice, systemic racism, usurious payday and title loans, banks charging exorbitant interest rates on credit cards, an unjust tax code, the immigration crisis, pharmaceutical companies distributing opiates like candy, global warming, and a runaway military-industrial complex.

- How has the issue of homosexuality touched your life?

- Since 1972, the United Methodist Church has maintained that "the practice of homosexuality is incompatible with Christian teaching." It has also maintained that pastors may not be "self-avowed, practicing homosexuals" and may not conduct ceremonies that celebrate same-sex weddings or unions. What are your thoughts on the United Methodist Church's official stance on homosexuality?

- Which of the other issues Mike lists concerns you the most? Why?

5. Thomas Long offered this prescient warning over a quarter-century ago:

> In a 1994 editorial in Theology Today, Thomas Long disclosed a conversation that he shared with a journalist who said, "American Christians ought to be scared as hell." What was the reason for this ominous warning from this seasoned journalist? He answered, "Little Christians are simply not growing up to be big Christians anymore."

- If Thomas Long is right and the problem is that little Christians are not growing up to be big Christians anymore, what is the answer?

6. Have the mightiest Protestants run out of "meaning" as the title of Kenneth Woodward's 1993 article proclaimed? If so, in what ways?

Group Lectio Divina:

Matthew 9: 35–38 (CEB)

> 35 Jesus traveled among all the cities and villages, teaching in their synagogues, announcing the good news of the kingdom, and healing every disease and every sickness. 36 Now when Jesus saw the crowds, he had compassion for them because they were troubled and helpless, like sheep without a shepherd. 37 Then he said to his disciples, "The size of the harvest is bigger than you can imagine, but there are few workers. 38 Therefore, plead with the Lord of the harvest to send out workers for his harvest."

- Pray: One group member opens with a brief, spoken prayer.

- Read: Another group member reads the passage aloud, slowly.

- Reflect: Group members spend one minute silently reflecting on the passage.

- Share: Each group member shares their answer to the question without explanation or comment: *"What word or phrase bubbled up to the surface or grabbed my attention?"*

- Read: Another group member reads the same passage aloud *from a different translation.*

- Reflect: For 3 minutes or so, group members silently reflect and jot down their answer to the question: *"Where does this passage touch my life experience?"*

- Share: Group members share their answers to the question (if they want).

- Read: A third group member reads the passage aloud *from yet another translation.*

- Reflect: For 3 minutes or so, group members jot down an answer to the question: *"From what I have heard and shared, who is God inviting me to be? How is God inviting me to change? What is God inviting me to do?"*

- Share: Each group member (who wants to) shares their answer, beginning: *"I believe God wants me to . . . "*

- Extended Sharing: Invite group members to share their responses to what others have shared. *How are you inspired or informed by their contributions to the discussion?*

- Silent Prayer: Each group member then silently prays for the person on his/her right, focusing on what that person expressed in the prior step. Each continues to pray for that person throughout the week.

WEEK 2: READ CHAPTERS 3 & 4

1. In chapter 3, Mike writes about how the book *Death of the Church* had a lasting impact on him. Other than the Bible, what book has had the most impact on your life, and in what ways?

2. Mike offers this withering critique of clergy:

   > *The laity come to church not for ecclesiastical disputes but to hear a liberating Word from God. They come to church to be encouraged, to be equipped, to be strengthened, so that they can be, like Teresa of Ávila wrote, "the hands and feet of Christ." Yet too often, what we clergy do is to fill the slot of committees of the church with names of people, engaging in a bait and switch. How often have we been the architects of a less than fulfilling deal?*

   - In what ways can you relate to this critique?

   - What have been your most fulfilling and least fulfilling experiences in the church?

3. In Chapter 4, Mike explores what healthy boundaries look like for clergy. He says this about Jesus: *"Jesus enforced boundaries that would get him fired by many American congregations."*

   - Are congregations guilty of expecting their clergy to be little more than a "quivering mass of availability", to borrow a phrase from Stanley Hauerwas?

   - What have you learned about saying no and setting boundaries?

4. Mike invites us to consider our investment in institutional Christianity:

   > *As preachers exit from the local church or when they draw near to retirement, many of them also wonder, how have they spent their light? Did they make a good choice investing in institutional Christianity? It is an investment that Jesus never made.*

   - How are you re-evaluating your investment in institutional Christianity these days?

- In 1786, at the age of 83, the founder of Methodism, John Wesley, wrote these haunting words in the pamphlet "Thoughts on Methodism": *"I am not afraid that the people called Methodists should ever cease to exist either in Europe or America. But I am afraid lest they should only exist as a dead sect, having the form of religion without the power. And this undoubtedly will be the case unless they hold fast both the doctrine, spirit, and discipline with which they first set out."* How do Wesley's words speak to this moment in the life of the church?

5. Have you ever wrestled with wanderlust, with second thoughts about the course of your life and your unactualized dreams? How do these often-quoted words—*"You're never too old to set another goal, or to dream a new dream"*—offer a needed perspective?

6. Mike writes about an experience early in his ministry when he is with his district superintendent just days after the death of his assigned mentor in ministry. Their conversation is interrupted by a phone call to the district superintendent. Mike learns that another minister has called to put his name in consideration for the opening at the church where his mentor had served. Mike comments rather wistfully, *"Looking back all these years later, I know how true it is that life moves onward; ceremonies are held, and gaps are filled."* How are these wise words to us who are still living?

7. In the fourth chapter, we learn about Barbara Brown Taylor's experience of the Divine Presence. When and/or where are you especially conscious of the Divine Presence?

Group Lectio Divina:

Acts 2:42–47 (CEB)

> 42 *The believers devoted themselves to the apostles' teaching, to the community, to their shared meals, and to their prayers. 43 A sense of awe came over everyone. God performed many wonders and signs through the apostles. 44 All the believers were united and shared everything. 45 They would sell pieces of property and possessions and distribute the proceeds to everyone who needed them. 46 Every*

*day, they met together in the temple and ate in their homes. They
shared food with gladness and simplicity. 47 They praised God and
demonstrated God's goodness to everyone. The Lord added daily to
the community those who were being saved.*

- Pray: One group member opens with a brief, spoken prayer.

- Read: Another group member reads the passage aloud, slowly.

- Reflect: Group members spend one minute silently reflecting on
  the passage.

- Share: Each group member shares their answer to the question
  without explanation or comment: *"What word or phrase bubbled
  up to the surface or grabbed my attention?"*

- Read: Another group member reads the same passage aloud from
  a different translation.

- Reflect: For 3 minutes or so, group members silently reflect and
  write down their answer to the question: "Where does this passage touch my life experience?"

- Share: Group members share their answers to the question (if
  they want).

- Read: A third group member reads the passage aloud from yet
  another translation.

- Reflect: For 3 minutes or so, group members write an answer to
  the question: "From what I have heard and shared, what is God
  inviting me to be? How is God inviting me to change? What is
  God inviting me to do?"

- Share: Each group member (who wants to) shares their answer,
  beginning: "I believe God wants me to . . . "

- Extended Sharing: Invite group members to share their responses
  to what others have shared. How are you inspired or informed by
  their contributions to the discussion?

- Silent Prayer: Each group member then silently prays for the person on his/her right, focusing on what that person expressed in
  the prior step. Each continues to pray for that person throughout
  the week.

WEEK 3: READ CHAPTERS 5 & 6

1. J. Christiaan Beker was one of the legendary professors at Princeton when Mike attended there. Who was one of your "legendary" teachers in school? What made them legendary?

2. In his book, *Paul, the Apostle*, Beker writes: *"Because the church is not an elite body separated from a doomed world, but a community placed in the midst of the cosmic community of creation, its task is not merely to win souls but to bear the burdens of creation to which it not only belongs, but to which it must also bear witness."* What do you think it means for the church to "bear the burdens of creation"? How is your church attempting to do this?

3. In contrast to the smart, the athletic, the beautiful, Mike offers a contrasting understanding of the best life: *"What God values, first and foremost, is faithfulness; living a soulful life that loves and values others; a life that treats all with the inherent dignity and worth that they deserve as children of God."*

    • When you think about someone, living or dead, who lives or lived the soulful life, who comes to mind? And what makes or made their life stand out as soulful?

    • What situations most challenge your capacity to treat "all with the inherent dignity and worth they deserve?"

4. Bruce Springsteen's *Born in the U.S.A* is about the troubled return home of a Vietnam veteran. The rousing chorus is actually a bitterly sarcastic response to the day-to-day realities of life for a vet who ten years later sums up his life this way: *"Down in the shadow of the penitentiary/ Out by the gas fires of the refinery/ I'm ten years burning down the road/ Nowhere to run ain't got nowhere to go."*

    • What is most troubling for you when you contrast our country's ideals with the day-to-day realities for so many?

    • Do you see signs or outposts of hope? Where?

5. Mike quotes the brilliant Albert Einstein, *"Imagination is more important than knowledge. Knowledge is limited whereas imagination*

embraces the world." And he laments: *"United Methodist congregations have far too often resisted embracing reawakened imagination in favor of the status quo."*

- In what ways have United Methodists and other mainline Protestant congregations "resisted embracing reawakened imagination?"
- When have you participated in a ministry that employed your best imaginative powers?

6. Writing about Hemingway's marital infidelity, Mike describes the cost: *"Seizing the day can bring a tidal wave of grief to others."*

- The New Living Translation of 1 Corinthians 13:4–5 reads: *"⁴ Love is patient and kind. Love is not jealous or boastful or proud ⁵ or rude. It does not demand its own way. It is not irritable, and it keeps no record of being wronged."* How do Paul's words here prod us to examine our hearts?

Group Lectio Divina

Hebrews 13:1–6 (CEB)

> *Keep loving each other like family. ² Don't neglect to open up your homes to guests, because by doing this some have been hosts to angels without knowing it. ³ Remember prisoners as if you were in prison with them, and people who are mistreated as if you were in their place. ⁴ Marriage must be honored in every respect, with no cheating on the relationship, because God will judge the sexually immoral person and the person who commits adultery. ⁵ Your way of life should be free from the love of money, and you should be content with what you have. After all, he has said, I will never leave you or abandon you. ⁶ This is why we can confidently say,*
>
> > *The Lord is my helper,*
> > *and I won't be afraid.*
> > *What can people do to me?*

- Pray: One group member opens with a brief, spoken prayer.

- Read: Another group member reads the passage aloud, slowly.

- Reflect: Group members spend one minute silently reflecting on the passage.

- Share: Each group member shares their answer to the question without explanation or comment: "What word or phrase bubbled up to the surface or grabbed my attention?"

- Read: Another group member reads the same passage aloud from a different translation.

- Reflect: For 3 minutes or so, group members silently reflect and write down their answer to the question: "Where does this passage touch my life experience?"

- Share: Group members share their answers to the question (if they want).

- Read: A third group member reads the passage aloud from yet another translation.

- Reflect: For 3 minutes or so, group members write an answer to the question: "From what I have heard and shared, what is God inviting me to be? How is God inviting me to change? What is God inviting me to do?"

- Share: Each group member (who wants to) shares their answer, beginning: "I believe God wants me to . . . "

- Extended Sharing: Invite group members to share their responses to what others have shared. How are you inspired or informed by their contributions to the discussion?

- Silent Prayer: Each group member then silently prays for the person on his/her right, focusing on what that person expressed in the prior step. Each continues to pray for that person throughout the week.

WEEK 4: READ CHAPTERS 7 & 8

1. When studying the possibility of a building campaign, Main Street United Methodist in Kernersville, NC rightly addressed the question of whether Kernersville "really needed another church with a gym."

What do you think? Can a gym distract a church from keeping the main thing the main thing? Can a gym be a faithful use of funds and space?

2. In her book, *Leaving Church*, Barbara Brown Taylor confesses she rarely, truly observed the sabbath. One of the challenges we face in discussing Sabbath-keeping is that we misunderstand it. In another book, *An Altar in the World*, Taylor describes Sabbath-keeping this way:

> *At least one day in every seven, pull off the road and park the car in the garage. Close the door to the toolshed and turn off the computer. Stay home, not because you are sick but because you are well. Talk someone you love into being well with you. Take a nap, a walk, an hour for lunch. Test the premise that you are worth more than you can produce – that even if you spent one whole day of being good for nothing you would still be precious in God's sight. And when you get anxious because you are convinced that this is not so – remember that your own conviction is not required. This is a commandment. Your worth has already been established, even when you are not working. The purpose of the commandment is to woo you to the same truth.*

- When was the last non-vacation day you spent being "good for nothing"? How did it feel?

- How does Taylor's description deepen your understanding of Sabbath-keeping?

3. Mike writes about Taylor: *"Released from the burden of running the institution, Taylor became more intentional, living her faith fully. By no longer having to defend the faith, she had the opportunity to revisit the faith."* Have you had an opportunity at some juncture in your life to revisit the faith? Has the pandemic been just such a juncture for you?

4. How does *The Message* translation of the Great Commission in Matthew 28 enlarge its meaning for you?

> *Therefore, go and make disciples of all nations, baptizing them in the name of the Father and of the Son and of the Holy Spirit, and teaching them to obey everything I have commanded you. (NIV)*

Go out and train everyone you meet, far and near, in this way of life, marking them by baptism in the threefold name: Father, Son, and Holy Spirit. Then instruct them in the practice of all I have commanded you. (Message)

5. Jacob wrestled with God and walked the rest of his days with a limp. In the same way, Mike suggests that "the preacher wrestles with and is marked by Otherness." What do you think it means to be marked by Otherness? And how is every follower of Jesus marked by Otherness?

6. Commenting on the story of the man born blind in John 9, Mike writes:

> *How often have we heard the trite expression on a preacher's lips of "Love the sinner and hate the sin?" Those who struggle with whatever the preacher has elevated do not feel that so-called love. They feel isolated and judged.*

- In the eyes of many non-Christians, Christians are known for how deeply we judge, not for how deeply we love. Is this perception valid? What has been your experience with judgmental Christians?

- We are all on a journey from judger to loving helper. How do you still struggle with judgmentalism?

Group Lectio Divina

Romans 12:3–8 (CEB)

> 3 *Because of the grace that God gave me, I can say to each one of you: don't think of yourself more highly than you ought to think. Instead, be reasonable since God has measured out a portion of faith to each one of you. 4 We have many parts in one body, but the parts don't all have the same function. 5 In the same way, though there are many of us, we are one body in Christ, and individually we belong to each other. 6 We have different gifts that are consistent with God's grace that has been given to us. If your gift is prophecy, you should prophesy in proportion to your faith. 7 If your gift is service, devote yourself to serving. If your gift is teaching, devote yourself to teaching. 8 If your gift is encouragement, devote yourself to encouraging.*

The one giving should do it with no strings attached. The leader should lead with passion. The one showing mercy should be cheerful.

- Pray: One group member opens with a brief, spoken prayer.

- Read: Another group member reads the passage aloud, slowly.

- Reflect: Group members spend one minute silently reflecting on the passage.

- Share: Each group member shares their answer to the question without explanation or comment: "What word or phrase bubbled up to the surface or grabbed my attention?"

- Read: Another group member reads the same passage aloud from a different translation.

- Reflect: For 3 minutes or so, group members silently reflect and write down their answer to the question: "Where does this passage touch my life experience?"

- Share: Group members share their answers to the question (if they want).

- Read: A third group member reads the passage aloud from yet another translation.

- Reflect: For 3 minutes or so, group members write an answer to the question: "From what I have heard and shared, what is God inviting me to be? How is God inviting me to change? What is God inviting me to do?"

- Share: Each group member (who wants to) shares their answer, beginning: "I believe God wants me to ... "

- Extended Sharing: Invite group members to share their responses to what others have shared. How are you inspired or informed by their contributions to the discussion?

- Silent Prayer: Each group member then silently prays for the person on his/her right, focusing on what that person expressed in the prior step. Each continues to pray for that person throughout the week.

WEEK 5: READ CHAPTERS 9 & 10

1. In chapter nine, Mike recalls his friendship with Ruth, a rather cantankerous member of his congregation at his first appointment, Cavanaugh United Methodist Church in Fort Smith, Arkansas. In his visits with her, Ruth shares with Mike about her late husband who was a prisoner in a Japanese concentration camp during World War II suffering from PTSD after returning to the states. Mike writes, *"She cared for him and lived through his terrors. I wondered, what emotional price had she paid loving him as fiercely as she did?"* How would you describe the emotional price of love?

2. When Jesus taught people to love their neighbors as themselves (Mark 12:30–31) and treat others as they would be treated (Matthew 7:12), he was teaching people to seek the common good.

   • How do you seek the common good in your daily living?

   • Where do you see your life choices differing from "people who have been indoctrinated by a consumeristic society that they can have it their own way"?

3. Mike concludes, *"America still struggles with its original sin."* How are followers of Jesus and churches summoned to continue the unfinished work of dismantling racism - in our teaching, in our discipling, in our action in the community?

4. In chapter ten, Mike discusses the deep political divisions in our country. But he argues that a Christian's allegiance goes deeper than political loyalties:

   What matters for the Christian would be to vote for the candidate who most closely aligns with Jesus's values. Each person must weigh those sacred loyalties when entering the sanctuary of the voting booth.

   • What does it mean for followers of Jesus to declare that Jesus is Lord in the political arena?

5. Mike has lunch with Joe, an older parishioner in his first appointment in Fort Smith, Arkansas and the conversation turns to heroes.

- What characteristics of a hero do we uncover in Romans 15:1–2? *"We who are strong ought to bear with the failings of the weak and not to please ourselves. Each of us should please our neighbors for their good, to build them up." (Romans 15:1–2 NIV)*

- Who are the unsung heroes in your community?

6. Mike longs for a presidential candidate on the order of Jed Bartlet of *The West Wing.* One of Bartlet's more inspirational quotes speaks to the need for heroes in our country and world: *"The streets of heaven are too crowded with angels. But every time we think we've measured our capacity to meet a challenge, we look up and we're reminded that that capacity may well be limitless. This is a time for American heroes."* How might God be calling you to heroic action in these times?

7. Mike makes this observation about pastors and politics: *"One should not be surprised when a pastor tries to find a solution that makes all sides of the political spectrum satisfied. Yet, Jesus did not equivocate."* From your knowledge of Jesus, what are some things that Jesus did not equivocate- flip-flop, sit on the fence- on?

Group Lectio Divina

1 Timothy 1: 6–12 (NIV)

> *6 For this reason I remind you to fan into flame the gift of God, which is in you through the laying on of my hands. 7 For the Spirit God gave us does not make us timid, but gives us power, love and self-discipline. 8 So do not be ashamed of the testimony about our Lord or of me his prisoner. Rather, join with me in suffering for the gospel, by the power of God. 9 He has saved us and called us to a holy life—not because of anything we have done but because of his own purpose and grace. This grace was given us in Christ Jesus before the beginning of time, 10 but it has now been revealed through the appearing of our Savior, Christ Jesus, who has destroyed death and has brought life and immortality to light through the gospel. 11 And of this gospel I was appointed a herald and an apostle and a teacher. 12 That is why I am suffering as I am. Yet this is no cause for shame, because I know whom I have believed, and am convinced that he is able to guard what I have entrusted to him until that day.*

- Pray: One group member opens with a brief, spoken prayer.

- Read: Another group member reads the passage aloud, slowly.

- Reflect: Group members spend one minute silently reflecting on the passage.

- Share: Each group member shares their answer to the question without explanation or comment: "What word or phrase bubbled up to the surface or grabbed my attention?"

- Read: Another group member reads the same passage aloud from a different translation.

- Reflect: For 3 minutes or so, group members silently reflect and write down their answer to the question: "Where does this passage touch my life experience?"

- Share: Group members share their answers to the question (if they want).

- Read: A third group member reads the passage aloud from yet another translation.

- Reflect: For 3 minutes or so, group members write an answer to the question: "From what I have heard and shared, what is God inviting me to be? How is God inviting me to change? What is God inviting me to do?"

- Share: Each group member (who wants to) shares their answer, beginning: "I believe God wants me to . . ."

- Extended Sharing: Invite group members to share their responses to what others have shared. How are you inspired or informed by their contributions to the discussion?

- Silent Prayer: Each group member then silently prays for the person on his/her right, focusing on what that person expressed in the prior step. Each continues to pray for that person throughout the week.

WEEK 6: READ CHAPTERS 11,12 & EPILOGUE

1. Commenting on John the Baptist and his message of repentance, Mike writes:

   Sometimes the kindest thing you can do is to tell someone that they are traveling in the wrong direction and that the only way they can arrive at their desired destination is to turn around and go in the opposite direction.

   - This is sometimes referred to as the "last 10 percent," the stuff we often won't share with someone because it's hard to do. Can you think of an instance when "the last 10 percent" made a constructive difference in your life or the life of someone you know?

2. Mike throws out two questions that deserve our attention: *"What does John the Baptist's witness of living simply in a self-imposed exile say into my life? What does John's witness say to us American consumers who are devouring our world's resources at a frightening rate?"*

3. Mike suggests John the Baptist would have strong words to speak to the American Church and our "preoccupations with expansive and expensive church campuses."

   - What are some ways your church buildings or campuses are used that you are proud of?

   - In Lewis Carroll's Alice in Wonderland, the white queen says to Alice: "Why, sometimes I've believed as many as six *impossible things before breakfast.*" In a spirit of believing impossible things, what imaginative uses can you envision for your church campus?

4. Mike makes it clear that if he were Pope, he would mandate we hold the United Methodist denomination together. What are the pluses and minuses of staying together? What are the pluses and minuses of separating? Where do you stand?

5. On Palm Sunday 2021, Mike preaches on Mark 11:1–11, the account of Jesus's entry into Jerusalem on a donkey, a symbol of peace. Marcus Borg and John Dominic Crossan argue in their book, *The Last Week,*

that this was a political counterdemonstration to Pontius Pilate who enters from the other side of town escorted by three thousand soldiers. Mike plays up the contrast: *"Two parades reflecting two very different kingdoms. One, where the Master lays down his life for his servants, and the other where Caesar and his representatives create rivers of suffering."*

- Should confrontation/protest/ counterdemonstrations have a place in our witness for Jesus?
- Jesus was a threat to the political powers of his day. How are his followers today challenged to declare and demonstrate their allegiance to a different kingdom?

6. In his epilogue, Mike shares the powerful story of a train ride in the summer of 1982 and his encounter with an elderly Roman Catholic priest from Germany. It was their mutual admiration for the life and witness of Dietrich Bonhoeffer that brought them together, erasing the age and language barriers that separated them. In his most famous work, *The Cost of Discipleship*, Bonhoeffer wrote, *"When Christ calls a man, he bids him come and die."* How do Bonhoeffer's words take practical shape in the life of a follower of Jesus?

7. Mike makes this confession, *"Those of us who serve the institutional church can sometimes get lost in the bricks, the mortar, the budget, the building campaign, and the worship and membership numbers."* How has this journey through Mike's book and your conversations together challenged your thinking about church and discipleship?

Group Lectio Divina

Matthew 7:13–14 (The Voice)

> 13 *There are two paths before you; you may take only one path. One doorway is narrow. And one door is wide. Go through the narrow door. For the wide door leads to a wide path, and the wide path is broad; the wide, broad path is easy, and the wide, broad, easy path has many, many people on it; but the wide, broad, easy, crowded path leads to death. 14 Now then that narrow door leads to a narrow*

road that in turn leads to life. It is hard to find that road. Not many people manage it.

- Pray: One group member opens with a brief, spoken prayer.
- Read: Another group member reads the passage aloud, slowly.
- Reflect: Group members spend one minute silently reflecting on the passage.
- Share: Each group member shares their answer to the question without explanation or comment: "What word or phrase bubbled up to the surface or grabbed my attention?"
- Read: Another group member reads the same passage aloud from a different translation.
- Reflect: For 3 minutes or so, group members silently reflect and write down their answer to the question: "Where does this passage touch my life experience?"
- Share: Group members share their answers to the question (if they want).
- Read: A third group member reads the passage aloud from yet *another translation.*
- Reflect: For 3 minutes or so, group members write an answer to the question: "From what I have heard and shared, what is God inviting me to be? How is God inviting me to change? What is God inviting me to do?"
- Share: Each group member (who wants to) shares their answer, beginning: "I believe God wants me to . . . "
- Extended Sharing: Invite group members to share their responses to what others have shared. How are you inspired or informed by their contributions to the discussion?
- Silent Prayer: Each group member then silently prays for the person on his/her right, focusing on what that person expressed in the prior step. Each continues to pray for that person throughout the week.

Joe A. Hamby is Director of Front Door Services for Roof Above in Charlotte, NC. He is also a United Methodist Deacon.

BIBLIOGRAPHY

Beker, J. Christiaan. *Suffering and Hope*. Philadelphia: Fortress 1987.

Berg, Scott A. *Max Perkins: Editor of Genius* New York: Random House, 2016.

Borg, Marcus J., and John Dominic Crossan. *The Last Week: A Day-by-Day Account of Jesus's Final Week in Jerusalem*. New York: HarperSanFrancisco, 2006.

Bonhoeffer, Dietrich. *The Cost of Discipleship*. New York: Macmillan, 1963.

Brammer, John Paul. "Billy Graham leaves a painful legacy for LGBTQ people," *NBC News* (February 22, 2018) https://www.nbcnews.com/feature/nbc-out/billy-graham-leaves painful-legacy-lgbtq-people-n850031.

Buechner, Frederick. *Peculiar Treasures: A Biblical Who's Who*. New York: HarperSanFrancisco, 1979.

———. *The Sacred Journey: A Memoir of Early Days*. New York: HarperSanFrancisco, 1982.

———. *Telling Secrets: A Memoir*. New York: HarperCollins, 1991.

Coles, Robert. *Harvard Diary: Reflections on the Sacred and the Secular*. New York: Crossroad, 1988.

Doctrines and Discipline of the Methodist Episcopal Church. New York: The Methodist Book Concern, 1928.

Edelstein, Jeff. "Albert Einstein was a Princeton genius. And math tutor." *The Trentonian* (March 12, 2015) https://www.trentonian.com/news/jeff-edelstein-albert-einstein-was-a-princeton-genius-and-math-tutor/article_0459ee9f-90bd-5df2-b9c0-be49f6c10e4c.html.

Feynman, Richard P. *"Surely You're Joking, Mr. Feynman!" Adventures of a Curious Character*. New York: W.W. Norton & Company, 1985.

Garry, Fred. G. "A Heavy Gold Chain." *First Presbyterian Church of Metuchen* (January 27, 2019) https://fpcweb.org/dev/sermons/a-heavy-gold-chain/.

Gehring, Michael J. *As the Broken White Lines Become One*. Eugene OR: Resource Publications, 2018.

———. *The Oxbridge Evangelist: Motivations, Practices, and Legacy of C.S. Lewis*. Eugene, OR: Cascade Books, 2017.

Goldberg, Jeffrey. "James Mattis Denounces President Trump, Describes Him as a Threat to the Constitution." *The Atlantic* (June 3, 2020) https://www.theatlantic.com/politics/archive/2020/06/james-mattis-denounces-trump-protests-militarization/612640/.

Greene, Graham. *The Power and the Glory*. Introduction by John Updike. New York: Penguin, 2015.

Hastings, Sara. "On March 14, All eyes in Princeton are on Einstein." *The Community News,* (February 28, 2018). https://communitynews.org/2018/02/28/all-eyes-on-einstein-princeton-pi-day/.

Hemingway, Ernest. *A Moveable Feast.* New York: Charles Scribner's Sons, 1964.

Herbert, George. *The Collar.* https://www.poetryfoundation.org/poems/44360/the-collar.

Herzog, Frederick. *God-Walk: Liberation Shaping Dogmatics.* Maryknoll, NY: Orbis, 1988.

Hinton, John. "President Trump should wear a mask during his visit to Winston-Salem, county Republican says." *Winston-Salem Journal* (September 8, 2020) https://journalnow.com/news/local/president-trump-should-wear-a-mask-during-his-visit-to-winston-salem-county-republican-says/article_551be240-ee3c-11ea-aaac-07490e3d44da.html.

Kelley, Dean M. *Why Conservative Churches Are Growing: A Study in Sociology of Religion With a New Preface for the ROSE Edition.* Mercer, GA: Mercer University Press, 1995.

Justice, Donald. *Men at Forty.* https://www.poetryfoundation.org/poetrymagazine/browse?contentId=30315.

Keillor, Garrison. "Those People Called Methodists." *Beliefnet.* https://www.beliefnet.com/columnists/bibleandculture/2007/02/garrison-keillor-on-those-people-called-methodists.html.

Lewis, C.S. *That Hideous Strength: A Modern Fairy-Tale for Grown-Ups.* New York: Macmillan, 1965.

———. *The Last Battle.* New York: HarperTrophy, 2000.

———. *Surprised by Joy: The Shape of My Early Life.* New York: Harcourt, Brace and Company, 1955.

Lochman, Jan M. "The Lord's Prayer in Our Time: Praying and Drumming." *The Princeton Seminary Bulletin* (Supplemental Issue 1992), No. 2, 5–19.

Long, Thomas G., "Beavis and Butt-Head Get Saved." *Theology Today* Vol. 51, No. 2 (July 1994) 199–203.

———. Email to Michael J. Gehring (April 6, 2021).

Mackin, Tom. "The Day Einstein Went Public." *The New York Times* (March 12, 1989) https://www.nytimes.com/1989/03/12/nyregion/new-jersey-opinion-day-einstein-went-public-tom-mackin-tom-mackin-lives-short.html?auth=login-email&login=emai.

Michener, James A. *The World is My Home: A Memoir.* New York: Random House, 1992.

Migliore, Daniel L. "J. Christiaan Beker: A Tribute (1924–1999)." *The Princeton Seminary Bulletin* Vol. 21: Issue 1 (2000) 96–98.

Miller, Hugh McHenry. "Christmas Past." *The Presbyterian Outlook.* (December 17, 2013).

Milton, John. *Sonnet 19: When I Consider How My Light Is Spent.* https://www.poetryfoundation.org/poems/44750/sonnet-19-when-i-consider-how-my-light-is-spent.

Mingels, Guido. Roland Nelles, Ralf Neukirch, Renê Pfister, and Marc Pitzke. "A Perfect Storm: Democracy on the Defensive in Trump's America." *Der Spiegel* (June 6, 2020) https://www.spiegel.de/international/world/a-perfect-storm-democracy-on-the-defensive-in-trump-s-america-a-00f31b18-b59e-4c45-a5f3-fde7c739d957.

Niebuhr, Reinhold. *Leaves from the Notebook of a Tamed Cynic.* Louisville, KY: Westminster/John Knox, 1980.

Obituary for Cintra Carter-Sander, *The East Hampton Star.* (September 3, 2020) https://www.easthamptonstar.com/obituaries/202093/cintra-carter-sander.

Ostling, Richard. "Those Mainline Blues: America's Old Guard Protestant churches confront an unprecedented decline." *Time* (May 22, 1989) 94–96.

Peterson, Eugene H., *The Message* in *The Essential Evangelical Parallel Bible: Updated Edition*. New York: Oxford University Press, 2004.

———. *Under the Unpredictable Plant: An Exploration in Vocational Holiness*. Grand Rapids: Eerdmans, 1992.

Rainer, Thom S. "Ten Reasons Why Your Church Members Are Ornery in the Pandemic." (July 26, 2020) https://churchanswers.com/blog/ten-reasons-why-your-church-members-are-ornery-in-the-pandemic/.

Rediger, G. Lloyd., *Clergy Killers: Guidance for Pastors of Congregations Under Attack*. Louisville, KY: Westminster/John Knox, 1997.

Regele, Mike and Mark Schulz. *Death of the Church*. Grand Rapids: Zondervan, 1995.

Stetzer, Ed. "If it doesn't stem its decline, mainline Protestantism has just 23 Easters left." *The Washington Post* (April 28, 2017). www.washingtonpost.com/news/acts-of-faith/wp/2017/04/28/if-doesnt-stem-its-decline-mainline-protestantism-has-just-23-easters-left/?utm_term=.7f8eb9396b4.

Taylor, Barbara Brown. *Learning to Walk in the Dark*. New York: HarperOne, 2014.

———. *Leaving Church: A Memoir of Faith*. New York: HarperColllins, 2006.

———. *The Preaching Life*. Cambridge, MA: Cowley Publications, 1993.

Templeton, Charles. *An Anecdotal Memoir*. Toronto: McClelland and Stewart, 1983.

Wallis, Jim. *America's Original Sin: Racism, White Privilege, and the Bridge to a New America*. Grand Rapids: Brazos, 2016.

Weems, Lovett H. Jr. *Focus: The Real Challenges That Face the United Methodist Church*. Nashville: Abingdon, 2011.

Wilke, Richard B. *And Are We Yet Alive? The Future of the United Methodist Church*. Nashville: Abingdon, 1986.

Willimon, William H., *Pastor: The Theology and Practice of Ordained Ministry*. Nashville: Abingdon, 2016.

Willimon, William H., and Robert L. Wilson, *Rekindling the Flame: Strategies for a Vital United Methodism*. Nashville: Abingdon, 1987.

Woodward, Bob. *Rage*. New York: Simon & Schuster, 2020.

Woodward, Kenneth L., "Dead End for the Mainline? The Mightiest Protestants are running out of Money, Members and Meaning." *Newsweek* (August 9, 1993) 46–48.

Woodward, Kenneth L. with Patricia King, Peter McKillop and Anne Underwood, "From 'Mainline' to Sideline: Once the religious establishment, liberal Protestants are losing their sheep." *Newsweek* (December 22, 1986) 54-56.

Wright, N.T. *God and the Pandemic: A Christian Reflection on the Coronavirus and Its Aftermath*. Grand Rapids: Zondervan, 2020.

Yeats, William Butler. *The Second Coming*. https://www.poetryfoundation.org/poems/43290/the-second-coming.

Made in the USA
Columbia, SC
20 February 2022

56541674R00093